CAMPAIGN • 257

SALERNO 1943

The Allies invade southern Italy

ANGUS KONSTAM

ILLUSTRATED BY STEVE NOON
Series editor Marcus Cowper

First published in Great Britain in 2013 by Osprey Publishing,
Midland House, West Way, Botley, Oxford OX2 0PH, UK
43-01 21st Street, Suite 220B, Long Island City, NY 11101, USA
E-mail: info@ospreypublishing.com

ISBN: 978 1 78096 249 8
E-book ISBN: 978 1 78096 250 4
E-pub ISBN: 978 1 78096 251 1

Editorial by Ilios Publishing Ltd, Oxford, UK (www.iliospublishing.com)
Index by Marie-Pierre Evans
Typeset in Myriad Pro and Sabon
Maps by Bounford.com
3D bird's-eye view by The Black Spot
Battlescene illustrations by Steve Noon
Originated by PDQ Media, Bungay, UK
Printed in China through Worldprint Ltd.

13 14 15 16 17   10 9 8 7 6 5 4 3 2 1

ARTIST'S NOTE

EDITOR'S NOTE

Unless otherwise indicated, all the images come from the Stratford Archive.

THE WOODLAND TRUST

Osprey Publishing are supporting the Woodland Trust, the UK's leading
woodland conservation charity, by funding the dedication of trees.

Key to military symbols

Army Group	Army	Corps	Division	Brigade	Regiment	Battalion
Company/Battery	Platoon	Section	Squad	Infantry	Artillery	Cavalry
Airborne	Unit HQ	Air defence	Air Force	Air mobile	Air transportable	Amphibious
Anti-tank	Armour	Air aviation	Bridging	Engineer	Headquarters	Maintenance
Medical	Missile	Mountain	Navy	Nuclear, biological, chemical	Ordnance	Parachute
Reconnaissance	Signal	Supply	Transport movement	Rocket artillery	Air defence artillery	

Key to unit identification

Unit identifier | Parent unit
Commander
(+) with added elements
(-) less elements

CONTENTS

The Allied invasion of southern Italy

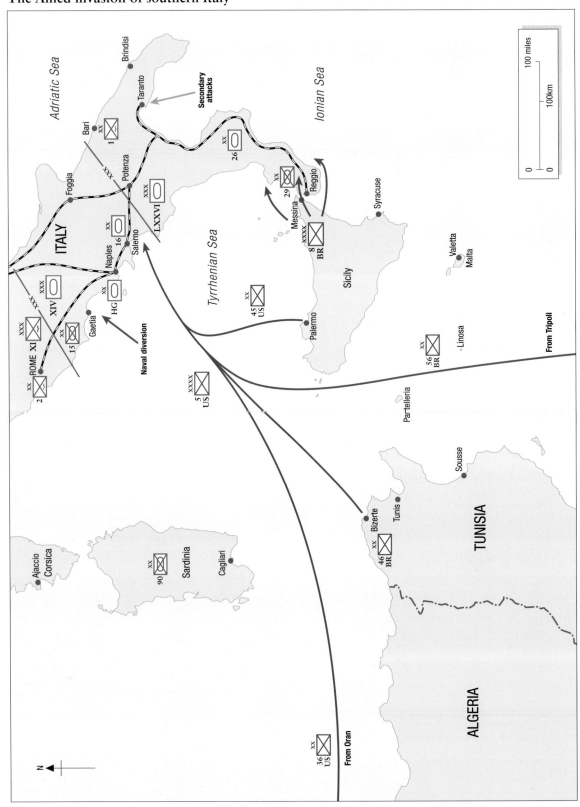

INTRODUCTION

In September 1943 the Allies invaded Italy, an operation which marked the start of the Western Allied assault on Hitler's 'Festung Europa' (Fortress Europe). It was an operation that nearly didn't succeed. In what became known as Operation *Avalanche*, an Anglo-American invasion force of more than 80,000 men was landed on the beaches of the Gulf of Salerno, to the south of Naples. The plan was to establish a bridgehead and then to drive north to capture Naples, whose port could then be used to support the Allied drive up the Italian Peninsula. The Italian army had just surrendered, and many in the invasion ships thought that resistance would be relatively light. They were proved wrong. The invasion was bitterly contested, and what followed was one of the hardest-fought campaigns of the war.

For obvious reasons no photographs were taken of the first waves of American troops who landed at Salerno. They landed before dawn and were under fire. This shot was taken of GIs of a supporting wave, wading ashore from an LCVP (Landing Craft, Vehicle and Personnel).

This attitude – that the invasion was little more than a clearing operation – permeated Hitler's headquarters as well as those of the Allies. He considered Italy to be indefensible, and his advisors recommended that he withdraw his German troops to the Po Valley, to avoid them becoming trapped in the Italian Peninsula. It was Generalfeldmarschall Albert Kesselring who persuaded him that Italy could be held, and that the fighting there would tie up Allied formations which might otherwise be deployed in the impending invasion of north-west Europe. Therefore, as one side looked optimistically to a potentially easy victory, their opponents took over abandoned Italian defences and grimly prepared for the fight of their lives.

An amphibious invasion is one of the most difficult military operations to carry out. Regardless of how much planning and logistical preparation is made, there are so many intangible factors that organizers are often unable to predict the outcome. If the invasion force manages to establish a viable bridgehead, then the operation often becomes a race to bring in reinforcements. If the defenders can be reinforced faster than the invaders, then they might well be able to launch a counter-attack designed to drive the enemy back to their ships. This is exactly the situation that developed at Salerno, and when it came the German counter-attack very nearly succeeded. For ten days the fate of the Allied invasion of Italy – even the fate of Italy herself – hung in the balance, as both sides vied for control of the narrow, beleaguered beachhead. The Salerno campaign was a critical moment in the struggle against Nazi Germany.

THE STRATEGIC SITUATION

The landing of an Allied army on the Italian mainland almost never happened. In January 1943, President Roosevelt and Prime Minister Churchill met in Casablanca to determine the strategy of the next phase of the war. At that moment Allied forces were poised to overrun the last Axis foothold in Tunisia, and the big question was what to do next. First, they clarified their war aims – to force an 'unconditional surrender' on Germany. Then they talked about strategy. Roosevelt and his senior commanders favoured the harbouring of resources for an Allied invasion of north-west Europe.

The British were less keen, feeling the time wasn't right. Churchill preferred delaying a cross-Channel invasion for a year or more, and instead to devote resources to the Mediterranean. Having fought them since June 1940, Britain preferred to knock Italy out of the war first, and thereby safeguard her sea communications with India and the Middle East. In the end, Churchill got his way, with several provisos, in return for a promise of greater British involvement in the war in the Pacific.

A Sherman tank of the US 2nd Armored Division entering Palermo on 22 July 1943. The capture of Sicily paved the way for the Allied invasion of the Italian mainland, despite the reluctance of Eisenhower and other American planners to venture onto the Italian mainland.

The decision was made that after forcing the surrender of the Germans in Tunisia, the Allies would invade Sicily. This would bring immediate strategic benefits, such as placing the Italian mainland in range of Allied bombers, and it would safeguard the transit of Allied convoys through the Western Mediterranean. However, General Eisenhower, the Supreme Allied Commander in the Mediterranean Theatre, had reservations about what he saw as a potentially open-ended commitment to a war in Italy. He demanded and received assurances that any offensive in the Mediterranean would be conducted in a limited way, and would not prevent the transfer of troops and supplies from what he saw as the more important operation – the assault on north-west Europe.

In the end Operation *Husky* was a success. On 10 July 1943 the Allies established beachheads on the southern and south-eastern coasts of the island, and then drove north and west, pushing the Germans and their unenthusiastic Italian allies before them. Italian units surrendered en masse, and, although German resistance hardened around the volcanic slopes of Mount Etna, by 17 August the Allies had captured the port of Messina in the north-east corner of Sicily and the island lay entirely in their hands. The only negative aspect was the fact that over 60,000 German troops had managed to escape from the island as they and their equipment were ferried to safety across the Straits of Messina under cover of darkness. Still, as well as securing the Allied lines of communication, the capture of Sicily had also exerted considerable moral and physical pressure on the Italian state. Mussolini's Fascist regime had collapsed, and there were clear signs that the interim Italian government had no stomach for continued war.

More than anything else it was this political situation that turned Eisenhower's fears of an open-ended commitment into a reality. Even before *Husky*, at the Washington Conference in May, Churchill had persuaded Roosevelt that Italy should be knocked out of the war, and that, while the vital attack against 'Festung Europa' would be a cross-Channel invasion, there was also a possibility that a successful capture of Sicily could be exploited by extending the conflict to encompass the Italian mainland. This would serve to tie down German troops, it would improve the strategic situation in the Mediterranean, and it would demonstrate a commitment to the West's Soviet allies that they meant business. Therefore, against his better judgement, Eisenhower gave the order to begin drawing up plans for an invasion of the Italian mainland.

Meanwhile, the political situation was changing rapidly. Mussolini was voted out of office on the night of 24–25 July, and the following morning King Victor Emmanuel III ordered the arrest of the Italian dictator.

Landing ships of TG 81.3 – the Landing Craft Group of the Southern Attack Force – en route to the Gulf of Salerno on 8 September. Barrage 'blimps' offer some protection from air attack, but the group was also escorted by a powerful force of destroyers.

A new government was formed under the leadership of Marshal Badoglio, and on 15 August – two days before the Allied capture of Messina – Badaglio's representative General Castellano approached the British Embassy in Madrid, and told the astonished staff there that if the Allies landed in Italy his government would be prepared to switch sides.

Castellano was told that the Allies would demand a military capitulation, the surrender of the Italian fleet and an immediate armistice. On 31 August Castellano flew to Sicily, and told the Allies that with a German army stationed in their country the Italian government was reluctant to announce an armistice for fear of German reprisals. They would only consider such an announcement if the Allies would follow up their declaration with an immediate invasion in strength, ideally in the vicinity of Rome.

The modern waterfront of Salerno, looking south from the town's old harbour. In the distance is the outlying spur of the Piscentini Hills which almost reaches the sea near Mercatello. On the extreme right is the most northerly of the British landing beaches, 6 miles down the coast from this viewpoint.

The Tempio di Nettuno (Temple of Neptune) formed part of the Greco-Roman ruins at Paestum which were defended by German machine-gunners and snipers on D-Day. After the battle the temple was used as the headquarters of the US 40th Port Battalion, responsible for the offloading of supplies.

Even while Operation *Husky* was taking place, Allied planners began considering where they might launch an amphibious assault. The Adriatic coast was ruled out as it was too far from Allied air bases, and any invasion fleet would have to run the gauntlet of enemy air attacks. Most of the potential landing sides were on beaches close to Naples or Rome, from the beaches north of Anzio to the Gulf of Salerno. Other possible sites were identified around the 'toe' and 'heel' of southern Italy. The more northerly invasion sites offered the most substantial strategic rewards if the landing succeeded, but they also placed the beaches far from the Allied airfields in Sicily, and aircraft would only have a few minutes patrol time there before they were forced to head home. There also weren't enough aircraft carriers available to counter this lack of air cover.

A landing on the southern coast of Italy was largely free of risk, but it offered few strategic advantages. The invaders would have to march up the whole length of the Italian peninsula, and the rugged terrain of Calabria meant that the Germans could impose lengthy delays to any advance – buying time for reinforcements to reach the theatre from the north. Operations *Barracuda*, *Gangway* and *Mustang* all involved landings in the Bay of Naples, but these plans were abandoned as they were deemed too risky, both through a lack of suitable beaches and the fact that the Germans could bring in reinforcements faster than the Allies could.

Operation *Musket*, involved the landing of General Clark's Fifth US Army at Taranto, supported by a drop by the US 82nd Airborne Division. This too was discarded, although it was later resurrected and modified as a means of inserting the British 1st Airborne Division into Apulia. This plan became known as Operation *Slapstick*. Operations *Buttress* and *Goblet* involved sealing off the 'toe' of Italy, by landing elements of General Montgomery's Eighth Army in Calabria. These too were abandoned in favour of Operation *Baytown*, the crossing of the Straits of Messina.

The next idea was for a parachute landing of the 82nd Airborne Division around Naples (Operation *Giant I*). If this wasn't deemed suicidal enough, the planners then became concerned about protecting the Italian government, and devised Operation *Giant II*, a *coup de main* to seize Rome. The main aim of both of these airborne operations was to prevent German troops from reaching the main amphibious landing area further to the south – somewhere around Naples or Salerno. Worryingly, *Giant II* almost took place, but fortunately common sense prevailed and the mission was cancelled. In the end, the 82nd Airborne Division was able to modify the airlift part of these plans when they were called upon to drop in the Salerno area, in support of the beleaguered Allied land forces.

By now it was clear that two factors favoured an immediate intervention in Italy. First, the political situation was extremely favourable, but the longer the Allies delayed a landing the less enthusiastic the Italian government might become, and the greater the chance that the Germans would discover their intentions. Second, the German units in southern Italy who had fought in Sicily were still short of men and equipment, and it would take time before they were brought back up to a full state of readiness. A normally cautious Montgomery advocated an immediate crossing into Calabria, to establish himself in the Italian 'toe' before the Germans could react.

By the end of August Eisenhower had reached his fateful decision. He decided to make his move by launching not one amphibious invasion but two. The first would be an amphibious crossing of the Straits of Messina and a landing around Reggio di Calabria by XIII Corps of the Eighth Army. This was Operation *Baytown*, which took place on 3 September. The Germans offered little in the way of resistance – in fact when the crossing took place the bulk of their forces in Calabria were in the process of retreating further inland.

The landing craft used during this operation would then be transferred to Clark's Fifth US Army, and would be used for the main event – Operation *Avalanche* – the landing of Clark's army on the shores of the Gulf of Salerno. This was scheduled to take place on 9 September. A hastily arranged adjunct was Operation *Slapstick*,

General Alexander (right) visited the Salerno battlefield on 15 September. Here he and Lt. Gen. Clark (centre) survey the battlefield from the vantage point of a viaduct spanning Highway 18 near Mercatello. They are accompanied by Lt. Gen. McCreery.

the seaborne landing of the 1st British Airborne Division in Taranto, which took place at the same time as the Salerno landings.

The Gulf of Salerno had been chosen because it lay just within the range of Allied air cover, its waters were well suited to an amphibious invasion and the beaches at its eastern coast made a perfect landing place. Planners noted there were plenty of small roads which would help a rapid exploitation of the beachhead, while the small port of Salerno anchoring the north-east corner of the gulf would make a useful interim supply base. The immediate hinterland behind the beaches was spacious enough to hold supply dumps and troop staging areas, and there was even a small airfield there, which could be used to provide air cover for the beachhead.

The only real drawback was that the flat coastal plain of Salerno was ringed by mountains, which would give German artillery observers a grandstand view of the beachhead. In effect it resembled a giant amphitheatre, with the Allies being the actors and the Germans the audience. Worse still, unless the Allies could seize the passes through the mountains to the north before the Germans, then they would face a hard task advancing through these defiles to reach Naples. While Clark was undoubtedly aware of the importance of this high ground, occupying the passes before the Germans did would represent a real challenge to him and his men. Just as importantly, the high ground also dominated the roads leading to the south and west, which the Allies hoped to exploit in order to secure the rest of the region.

The plan was for both armies to push inland, and while Clarke secured the vital port of Naples, Montgomery would clear the southern portion of the Italian peninsula and take the town of Foggia, with its strategically important cluster of airfields. By the time the two armies linked up, all of southern Italy would be under Allied control, supplies would be arriving through Naples, and Alexander's two armies would be poised for a drive northwards towards Rome. On paper it all made perfect sense.

The same day that Montgomery landed in Calabria, Marshal Badaglio agreed to the armistice, but wanted to make his own decision on the timing of the announcement. Unfortunately for him, Eisenhower was now working to a tight timetable, and, under instructions from Washington and London, he publicly announced the Italian capitulation on the evening of 8 September. At that moment the troops of four Allied infantry divisions were at sea, and were due to arrive off Salerno the following morning. There was widespread rejoicing in the troopships, and many hoped the landing would be unopposed. Unfortunately for them, the Germans were quick to react. Following a pre-arranged plan the German units in Italy moved quickly to disarm the troops of their former ally, and to take over their bases, fortifications and airfields. That night German troops took over the Italian beach defences and coastal gun batteries overlooking the Gulf of Salerno. When dawn came the Germans would be ready and waiting.

A German artillery observation team in action off the Salerno beachhead. The ability of German spotters to overlook the landing beaches was a major factor in the Allied obsession with the capture of the high ground around Altavilla and 'White House Hill'.

CHRONOLOGY

3 September	Operation *Baytown* – crossing of the Straits of Messina.
5 September	US 36th Division leaves Oran.
6 September	British 46th Division leaves Bizerta.
	British 56th Division leaves Tripoli.
7 September	US 45th Division leaves Palermo.
8 September	Rendezvous of convoys west of beachhead.
	Announcement of Italian capitulation.

Thursday 9 September (D-Day)

0320hrs	Ranger and Commandos land at Maiori and Vietri.
0330hrs	US 36th Division begins landing near Paestum.
0335hrs	British troops begin landing south of Salerno.
0700hrs	Commandos occupy Dragonea and Cava.
	Paestum captured.
0800hrs	German counter-attack south of Paestum.
	Capture of Magazenno strongpoint.
1000hrs	Attack on Montecorvino Airfield.

1100hrs	Heavy fighting on Dragonea Hill – lasts all day.
1200hrs	US Rangers capture Chiunzi Pass.
1700hrs	British 56th Division advance on Battipaglia halted.
1800hrs	Capaccio captured.
1900hrs	Lower slopes of Mt Soprano cleared.
	Operation *Slapstick* – capture of Taranto.

Friday 10 September (D+1)

0600hrs	German counter-attack west of Battipaglia.
0630hrs	Guards Brigade assault UK 'Tobacco Factory'.
0800hrs	British patrols enter Salerno.
1100hrs	British ejected from Battipaglia.
1200hrs	US 45th Division lands at Paestum.
1400hrs	Summit of Mt Soprano captured.
1700hrs	Salerno cleared of Germans.
1830hrs	Fighting along Tusciano River and Montecorvino Airfield.
2000hrs	Albanella captured.
	Eighth Army reaches Catanzaro.

Saturday 11 September (D+2)

0800hrs	Start of major German counter-attack near Tusciano River.
0900hrs	USS *Philadelphia* badly damaged in air attack.
0930hrs	US 36th Division advances up Sele Valley.
1100hrs	Fighting along river Calore – lasts all day.
1200hrs	Americans enter Altavilla.
1230hrs	German counter-attack around 'Hospital Hill'.
1400hrs	Attack on US Tobacco Factory repulsed.
	German attack on La Molina Pass – fighting lasts all afternoon.
1600hrs	British 46th Division thrown back to 'White House Hill'.
1700hrs	Heavy fighting along Tusciano River.
2130hrs	Second Guards Brigade attack on UK 'Tobacco Factory' repulsed.
	Airstrip opened near Paestum.

Sunday 12 September (D+3)

0500hrs	German attack on 'Hospital Hill'.
0600hrs	Heavy fighting in hills above Altavilla.
0800hrs	The Rangers repulse attack on Chiunzi Pass.
0900hrs	US 36th Division occupies Persano.
	US 45th Division assaults US Tobacco Factory.
1000hrs	Heavy fighting around 'White House Hill'.
1300hrs	German counter-attack – US Tobacco Factory recaptured.
1700hrs	US Tobacco Factory recaptured by Americans.
2000hrs	Major German attack clears the British from 'Hospital Hill'.

Monday 13 September (D+4) 'Black Monday'

0500hrs	Heavy fighting around Altavilla.
0530hrs	Major air raid on fleet – Hospital Ship *Newfoundland* sunk.
0630hrs	Commandos driven from Dragonea Hill – recaptured at 1430hrs.
0900hrs	Americans resume advance up Sele Valley.
1100hrs	Guards Brigade attacked around Bellizi.
1400hrs	Start of German counter-attack.
1500hrs	Persano recaptured by Germans.
	German attack on Fosse Bridge repulsed.
1530hrs	Germans recapture US Tobacco Factory.
1830hrs	German drive over La Cosa stream repulsed.
1930hrs	Clark calls emergency meeting with Dawley.
2355hrs	Elements of 82nd Airborne drop within VI Corps perimeter.

Tuesday 14 September (D+5)

0530hrs	German attack on La Cosa positions repulsed.
0600hrs	German attack towards Bivio Cioffi.
	Major German assault on 'White House Hill' – 'The Pimple' captured.
0700hrs	German attacks launched from US Tobacco Factory.
0730hrs	German attack on Fosse Bridge repulsed.

1230hrs	German assault on Bivio Cioffi repulsed.	
1300hrs	German attack on Monte San Chirico repulsed.	
1700hrs	British assault on UK 'Tobacco Factory' repulsed.	
2130hrs	German assault on La Calore position repulsed.	
2300hrs	Elements of 82nd Airborne land within VI Corps perimeter, and at Avellino.	

Wednesday 15 September (D+6)

0600hrs	Landing of 7th Armoured Division.
0830hrs	General Alexander tours battlefield.
1000hrs	German attack on 'White House Hill'.
1500hrs	US 36th Division advances front line towards Persano.
1830hrs	Commandos briefly recapture 'The Pimple'.
2000hrs	Commando assault on 'The Pimple' repulsed.

Thursday 16 September (D+7)

0700hrs	German attack on Fosso Bridge repulsed.
1400hrs	German assaults on Piegollele and 'Commando Hill'.
1420hrs	*Warspite* badly damaged in air raid.
1700hrs	82nd Airborne assault on Altavilla repulsed.
2000hrs	Link-up between VI Corps and leading elements of Eighth Army at Vallo.

Friday 17 September (D+8)

0700hrs	82nd Airborne attack on Altavilla – village captured at 1500hrs.
1500hrs	General Eisenhower tours battlefield.
1700hrs	German AOK 10 ordered to withdraw troops south of Salerno.
2200hrs	Germans abandon Battipaglia.

Saturday 18 September (D+9)

0200hrs	Commandos recapture 'The Pimple' but are forced to withdraw.
0600hrs	US 3rd Infantry Division lands at Paestum.
1000hrs	Scots Guards reoccupy UK 'Tobacco Factory' and Bellizi.
1200hrs	British 56th Division captures Battipaglia.
1800hrs	US 45th Division reoccupies US Tobacco Factory.

Sunday 19 September (D+10)

0030hrs	Persano reoccupied by US 36th Division.
0800hrs	Clark relieves Dawley of his command.
1400hrs	Ponte Sele captured by US 45th Division.
1700hrs	German rearguard encountered at Oliveto.
23 September	X Corps begins advance towards Naples.
1 October	Naples liberated.

OPPOSING COMMANDERS

GERMAN COMMANDERS

Generalfeldmarschall Albert Kesselring (1881–1960), or 'Smiling Albert' as he was known, was a Bavarian, the son of a schoolteacher. He joined the army as an artillery cadet in 1905, and in 1914 he took part in the German invasion of France. By 1917 he was posted to the staff as an artillery specialist, and ended the war as a *Hauptmann*. He remained in the army during the Weimar period, and in 1930 he became an *Oberstleutnant*. In 1933 he was transferred to the Reich Air Ministry, and given the rank of *Oberst*. He also learned to fly. By 1936 he had become a *Generalleutnant*, and was heavily involved in the rapid expansion of the Luftwaffe. He then became the Luftwaffe's Chief-of-Staff, under Hermann Göring, before being promoted to *General der Flieger* (Air Force General) in August 1938.

Despite originally being a Luftwaffe officer, Generalfeldmarschall Albert Kesselring was charged with masterminding the defence of Italy in 1943. It was his decision to contest the landings that led directly to the aggressive stance taken by the Germans at Salerno.

During the invasion of Poland in 1939 Kesselring supervised the provision of close air support for the army, and during the invasion of France in 1940 he commanded Luftflotte 2, which was charged with gaining air superiority and supporting the ground offensive. He went on to command the formation during the Battle of Britain, which concentrated its efforts on conducting bombing raids, including the raid on Coventry. Following the invasion of the Soviet Union in June 1941 Kesselring's Luftflotte 2 supported the offensive, and was responsible for destroying over 2,500 Soviet aircraft during the opening week of the campaign. By winter Kesselring's pilots were flying over Moscow, but the ground offensive had stalled.

In November Kesselring was sent to the Mediterranean, where he was appointed as Commander-in-Chief South, or Theatre Commander. In this capacity he oversaw the bombing campaign against Malta, the massed air attacks against the Royal Navy's Mediterranean fleet and the insertion of a German combat force in

North Africa, to bolster the Italians there. Kesselring's priority was to supply his forces in North Africa, and to prevent the British from supplying their own forces, or their island fortress of Malta. Kesselring's ultimate failure to achieve this had more to do with British resolve and the Italian lack of it than his own strategic shortcomings. He fought well in Tunisia, despite the odds against him, and when the campaign there ended in failure he set about shoring up the defences of Sicily and the Italian mainland.

In Sicily Kesselring did what he could to halt the Allies, and then withdrew his German forces to safety over the Straits of Messina. This was something of a masterstroke, as it preserved the core of his mechanized forces and meant that he was able to react swiftly to the Allied invasion at Salerno. During the campaign there Kesselring realized the importance of the battle, and his troops came close to success. Inevitably he was defeated by geography – the advance of the Eighth Army from the heel and toe of Italy meant that he had little option but to withdraw. Despite his background as an air commander, Kesselring had an eye for ground, and he realised that

General der Panzertruppen Heinrich von Vietinghoff commanded the German AOK 10 throughout the Salerno campaign, and afterwards he was promoted by Adolf Hitler in recognition of his leadership and achievements during the battle.

in Italy – especially in winter – the terrain favoured the defender. After Salerno he successfully established a defensive line across the Italian peninsula and effectively halted the Allied advance there for almost six months.

Kesselring had a good working relationship with Hitler, and he wasn't afraid to contradict him, or make his own decisions. He also understood the Italian terrain better than Hitler and his Allied opponents. Hitler's advisors – including Rommel – told him that Italy was indefensible in the aftermath of Italy's surrender. Kesselring disagreed, and even threatened to resign if he was ordered to withdraw. Hitler changed his mind, Kesselring was allowed to stay and fight, and he then went on to prove Rommel wrong.

Generaloberst Heinrich von Vietinghoff (1887–1952) commanded the German Armeeoberkommando 10. He hailed from Mainz and was born into a military family. He joined the army in 1902, and served with Hessian infantry during World War 1, earning the Iron Cross (1st class) and becoming a *Hauptmann* in 1915. He remained in the army after the war, and by 1933 he had become an *Oberst*. In 1938 he was promoted to *Generalleutnant*, and given command of the 5. Panzer-Division, but shortly before the outbreak of war he was promoted again, and given XIII Armeekorps to command. He performed well during the Fall of France (1940), and he went on to command a Panzer corps in Russia. After participating in Operation *Barbarossa* and its immediate aftermath Vietinghoff was given command of Armeeoberkommando (AOK) 5 (the German Fifth Army) stationed in France.

He remained there until the Allied invasion of Sicily, at which point he was promoted to full general, sent to Italy, and given command of AOK 10. He therefore assumed command shortly before the Salerno landings, and in the few weeks of respite before the invasion began he worked tirelessly to reconstitute and re-equip the mechanized forces evacuated from Sicily. He also instituted the plan to take over Italian bases and coastal defences following the Italian surrender to the Allies. During the Salerno campaign Vietinghoff was well aware of the importance of containing the Allied beachhead, but he also had to juggle the fighting around Salerno with the need to slow down the advance of Montgomery as he advanced towards Salerno from the south. Vietinghoff was a highly competent commander, who did as well as he could given the difficult strategic situation he faced and the lack of resources put at his disposal.

General der Panzertruppen Traugott Herr commanded LXXVI Panzer Korps at Salerno. As well as masterminding the German counter-attack on 13 September, he was also responsible for delaying the advance of Montgomery from Calabria.

Vietinghoff's two corps commanders were both highly experienced tank men. **General der Panzertruppen Hermann Balck** (1897–1982), commanding XIV Panzer Korps, was the son of a Prussian general, and first experienced combat on the Western Front during World War 1. Balck remained in the army, and became an advocate of mechanized warfare. During the Fall of France in 1940 he commanded a motorized rifle regiment – part of the 1. Panzer-Division – and he subsequently commanded a Panzer regiment during the campaign in Greece and the Balkans. In May 1942 he was promoted to *Generalleutnant* and given command of the 11. Panzer-Division, which he led during the drive on Stalingrad. Later he commanded the Panzergrenadier-Division 'Grossdeutchland', before being promoted, and transferred to Italy to take command of XIV Panzer Korps.

The LXXVI Panzer Korps was commanded by **General der Panzertruppen Traugott Herr** (1890–1976). He was a Saxon who served on the Western Front during World War I. He was a machine-gun officer, and was both wounded and decorated during the conflict, ending the war as a *Leutnant*. He remained in the army, and from 1929 on he specialized in mechanized warfare. In 1939 he commanded a motorized infantry regiment, and in 1939–40 he took part in the fighting in Poland and France as part of the 13. Infanterie-Division (mot.) (re-designated a Panzer-Division in 1940).

He participated in Operation *Barbarossa*, and in November 1941 he was promoted and given command of what was now the 13. Panzer-Division, which fought on the Eastern Front throughout the winter and summer campaigns in southern Russia and the Caucasus in 1941–42. Herr was badly wounded in October 1942, and he only returned to service in June 1943, at which point he was promoted and sent to Italy to assume command of LXXVI Panzer Korps. Both Balck and Herr were experts in Panzer warfare, and could be relied upon to fight aggressively, and to use their initiative. Both were also far more experienced than their Allied counterparts.

ALLIED COMMANDERS

General Sir Harold Alexander (1891–1969) was born into an aristocratic family, and was educated at Harrow. He joined the Irish Guards in 1912, and served with them in 1914, before being wounded at Ypres. He rejoined the regiment in 1915, and during the battle of Loos he acted as a temporary battalion commander. He won the Military Cross at Loos, and the DSC at the Somme the following year. He commanded his battalion at Third Ypres and, although still a major, he ended the war commanding a Brigade of Guards. He then saw action during the Russian Civil War, before returning home to command his battalion. Alexander became a colonel in 1928, and attended the Imperial Defence College, where his teacher – the future Field Marshal Brooke – found him unimpressive.

He was sent to India, where he performed well in actions on the North-West Frontier, and by 1937 Alexander had been promoted to major-general, the youngest in the British Army. During the Fall of France Alexander commanded the 1st Infantry Division, and did well during the retreat and evacuation of Dunkirk. He was given command of a corps deployed in the north of England, but was soon placed in charge of the defences of the south-west, with promotion to lieutenant-general following in December 1940.

In early 1942 Alexander was knighted, promoted to general, and sent to Burma to oversee the defence of the region, but he was unable to prevent the Japanese from overrunning the country and forcing the Allies back to the Indian border. After the situation stabilized he was recalled to London, and from there he was sent to Cairo, to take over command of British forces in the Middle East. Alexander commanded Montgomery's British Eighth Army, and from February 1943 on he also commanded the American forces in the Mediterranean theatre. He proved adept with dealing with the comparatively inexperienced Americans – Omar Bradley subsequently praised Alexander's tact in handling the Americans, who gained in combat experience under his guidance. Following the Allied victory in Tunisia Alexander was given command of the 15th Army Group, which now consisted of Montgomery's British Eighth Army and the Seventh US Army, commanded by Lieutenant-General George S. Patton. Alexander commanded these forces during Operation *Husky* – the Allied invasion of Sicily, an operation that was judged a great success. However, the Allies proved unable to prevent the evacuation of many of the German troops (and much of their equipment) from Sicily – troops that would fight the Allies again around the Salerno

General Sir Harold Alexander commanded the 15th Army Group with diplomacy and competence during the Italian campaign, and was responsible for deciding how and when the invasions of Sicily and the Italian mainland would take place.

beachhead. After Sicily, and in preparation for Operation *Avalanche*, Lieutenant-General Mark Clark's Fifth US Army replaced the Seventh US Army.

During the Salerno campaign Alexander adopted a 'hands off' approach, leaving Clark and Montgomery to fight as they saw fit. His only intervention came at the height of the Allied counter-attack, when he stiffened Clark's resolve to hold the bridgehead. While Alexander has been criticized for this very lack of control, given the personalities of his two army commanders and the need to work with both American and British naval and air commanders Alexander saw his main role as one of diplomatic coordination. In this he proved an excellent choice as a theatre commander, and the equal of his counterpart 'Smiling Albert'.

Brought up in a military family, **Lieutenant-General Mark W. Clark** (1896–1984) was raised in Illinois, went to West Point, and served in France with the American Expeditionary Force during 1917–18. After being wounded he was transferred to staff duties, and remained in that role or as a training commander throughout most of the inter-war years. In August 1941 Lt. Col. Clark was given a two-rung promotion to brigadier-general, as part of the pre-war expansion of the US Army, and became the Assistant

General Bernard L. Montgomery (left) of the British Eighth Army and Lieutenant-General Mark W. Clark of the Fifth US Army had very different styles of leadership, but both were very conscious of the importance of good publicity on their military careers.

Chief-of-Staff, based in Washington, DC. His first taste of real command came in June 1942, when he was sent to Britain to take command of US II Corps. Within two months he was promoted again, this time to major-general, and named the Commanding General, Army Forces, European Theater of Operations. There his duties involved the planning of Operation *Torch*, the US landing in North Africa. In November he was promoted again, and as a lieutenant-general he was given command of the Fifth US Army. It has been claimed that his rapid promotion from lieutenant-colonel to lieutenant-general was largely due to his friendship with Generals Marshall and Eisenhower.

While Operation *Husky* – the Allied invasion of Sicily – was taking place Clark continued to plan Operation *Avalanche*, and so when he landed on the Salerno beachhead he was setting foot on a battlefield for the first time in a quarter of a century. Salerno also represented his first trial as a combat commander. He performed reasonably well when things were going according to plan, but his indecision during the German counter-attack has led to criticism of his abilities as a battlefield commander. In the end he blamed his subordinate Dawley for the near-disaster, and remained in command of the Fifth US Army until December 1944, and was

Lieutenant-General Richard McCreery of X Corps was a highly experienced and competent commander, but at Salerno he was hampered by two largely inexperienced British divisions, and a determined and very aggressive opponent.

then commander of the 15th Army Group. After the war he was criticized for his obsession with personal glory – personified in his 'race for Rome' – and for his vanity. Alexander though, found him a likeable subordinate and much easier to work with than Montgomery, his counterpart in command of the British Eighth Army. Then again, that could probably have been said about most Allied generals.

Vice-Admiral Henry K. Hewitt USN (1887–1972) commanded the naval task force. A native of New Jersey, Hewitt joined the navy in 1906 and commanded a destroyer escort during World War I. He ended the rank with a Navy Cross and the rank of commander. By 1939 Hewitt had become a rear-admiral, and specialized in amphibious warfare. He supervised the amphibious landings during Operation *Torch* – the American landing in North Africa – and he went on to command the Western Naval Task Force that managed the amphibious landings and naval support during Operation *Husky*. Clearly Hewitt was the ideal officer to undertake the same role during Operation *Avalanche*. He had an excellent working relationship with his naval superior Admiral Sir Andrew Cunningham RN, but he was less enthusiastic in his association with Air Marshal Coningham, and the two men clashed over the allocation of air resources to *Husky* and *Avalanche*.

Lieutenant-General Sir Richard McCreery (1898–1967) joined the cavalry in 1915, and survived the war despite being seriously wounded. He even won a Military Cross during the offensive of 1918. He remained in the army, and in 1930 he became a brigadier. He was an excellent horseman, and an accomplished polo player, but he also willingly embraced mechanization. During the Fall of France in 1940 he commanded an armoured brigade, and went on to serve as an armoured specialist on the staff of the Eighth Army. He was given command of the British X Corps shortly before Operation *Avalanche*, and during the Salerno campaign he acquitted himself well, and remained in charge of his corps until his promotion to the command of the Eighth Army in December 1944.

Major-General Ernest J. Dawley commanded the US VI Corps at Salerno, but after the battle Lt. Gen. Clark relieved him of his command – effectively making him a scapegoat for American shortcomings during the campaign.

The commander of the US VI Corps was **Major-General Ernest J. Dawley** (1887–1973). He was an artilleryman and a competent enough corps commander, even though Alexander described him as 'a broken reed'. In Sicily, Patton replaced him with Omar Bradley as a corps commander in the Seventh US Army, and so Dawley was transferred to Clark's Fifth US Army shortly before Operation *Avalanche*. Clark thought Dawley lacked the aggression he wanted from his leading US commander, and was put under pressure from Eisenhower to replace him, as the Supreme Allied Commander, Mediterranean also considered Dawley too weak to hold such an important post. Clark resisted until Dawley's lacklustre performance during the German counter-attack forced his hand. He deemed Dawley to be 'worn out', and replaced him with Major-General John P. Lucas, a man who was replaced in his turn during the battle for Anzio.

OPPOSING FORCES

GERMAN FORCES

By the time the Allies landed at Salerno the Germans had already been engaged against Montgomery's Eighth Army for the best part of a week. Although it had been badly mauled in Sicily, the German army facing the Allies in southern Italy was far from the spent force suggested by Allied intelligence reports. While it was still hard to make good the losses in men, equipment and supplies during the short Sicilian campaign, it remained a well-led, highly motivated and thoroughly professional force. Even more importantly, unlike the majority of Clark's Fifth US Army, the men of the German AOK 10 were battle-hardened soldiers who knew their job.

The 16. Panzer-Division was deployed on the Salerno plain, having moved there a few weeks before from the south-east coast of Italy. Originally formed in 1940, the division had been destroyed at Stalingrad, but it was reformed around a cadre of veterans in March 1943. It was superbly led, but it lacked tanks. One of its two Panzer battalions was absent and in the process of being re-equipped with the new Panther tank. The division's four *Kampfgruppen* had to hold their positions against the full might of Clark's army until reinforcements could reach them.

The Panzer-Division 'Hermann Göring' was a peculiar unit whose origins could be traced back to the mid-1930s. A Luftwaffe formation, it was effectively the private army of the Reichsmarshall, and was considered a 'politicized' – if not a fanatical – outfit. In 1943 it was deployed in Sicily where it suffered heavy losses. As Göring's pride and joy, it was one of the first in line when it came to reinforcements and new equipment. Therefore, during the time it had spent reforming near Naples the division had regained much of its combat effectiveness. Still, it was chronically short of tanks and vehicles. Generalleutnant Paul Conrath commanded the division during this period, but he was on

A German Stug III assault gun of the 16. Panzer-Division, photographed in action during the battle for the Salerno beachhead. While the location of the photograph hasn't yet been identified, it may possibly have been south of Paestum, beyond the river Solofrone.

German prisoners from Panzer-Division 'Hermann Göring'. These young soldiers wear tropical uniform, while the teenager on the right appears to wear a late-pattern paratrooper's smock. They were reportedly captured around Vietri on D-Day.

A German 88mm Flak gun belonging to the 16. Panzer-Division, pictured in action on 9 or 10 September, firing on the British landing beaches. These guns could be used as artillery pieces when required, and they scored several hits on landing craft during the opening phase of the battle.

The crew of a German 20mm quadruple Flak gun in action during the Salerno battle. These weapons were used to protect the German mechanized units from air attack during the fighting, but they could also be deployed in a ground role if occasion demanded.

leave when the Allies landed, and so command fell to Generalmajor Wilhelm Schmalz. His men fought with great zeal and were considered tough opponents by the British Commandos who faced them.

Generalleutnant Rodt's 15. Panzergrenadier-Division, the 'Siziliendivisionen', was another formation that lacked tanks and vehicles, having been formed in May 1943 from the remnants of the original Panzer division of the same name that had been destroyed in North Africa. It then participated in the Sicily campaign. It was stationed near Gaeta when the Allies landed, and had only begun the process of rebuilding its strength when it was ordered south to Salerno.

The 3. Panzergrenadier-Division had arrived in Italy three months earlier, and was stationed near Rome. Elements of this well-equipped unit were ordered south from Frascati to Naples, where they came under the control of AOK 10.

Finally the 29. Panzergrenadier-Division and the 26. Panzer-Division were in Calabria, the former unit having arrived there from Sicily a few weeks before. The 29th had begun life as an infantry division, before it was destroyed at Stalingrad. In March 1943 a cadre of survivors were sent to the 345. Infanterie-Division, which duly became the 29th. It was considered an effective formation, despite its lack of vehicles and equipment. As for the 26. Panzer-Division, it was raised in late 1942 from elements of the 23. Infanterie-Division, and had served as a garrison unit in France until it was sent to Italy in June 1943. Both units might have been short of equipment, but their soldiers were confident, experienced, highly trained and ready for battle. However, these battle-hardened troops failed to defeat the relatively green Allied formations commanded by Clark. At Salerno the arbiter of victory proved to be weight of artillery and naval bombardment rather than the experience of the individual combat soldier. Put simply, these German veterans had no answer to the overwhelming firepower available to the Allies.

During the brief Salerno campaign the Germans rarely deployed divisions in their entirety. Instead they formed temporary battlegroups (*Kampfgruppen*). For the sake of simplicity, if the composition of a *Kampfgruppe* changed during the fighting, these changes are noted in the text, rather than here.

ALLIED FORCES

For the most part the British and American divisions that spearheaded Operation *Avalanche* were largely untested on the battlefield. There were exceptions. The British Commando Brigade and, to a lesser extent, the US Rangers had already seen action, and their high level of training, motivation and combat readiness made them exceptional fighters. Their leaders were also more willing to use their initiative than most regular infantry commanders, and so these formations – particularly the Commandos – were used extensively during the campaign. They also suffered heavy casualties in the process.

US Rangers emerge from a smokescreen, while fighting in the hills around Chiunzi Pass. The Rangers succeeded in holding this key objective throughout the battle, despite attempts by Panzer-Division 'Hermann Göring' to recapture it.

Similarly the paratroopers of the US 82nd 'All American' Airborne Division were well trained and relatively experienced. They had seen extensive action in both Tunisia and Sicily, and were used to operating both in small groups and in larger formations. They had made combat jumps before, and in Operation *Avalanche* they would serve as a useful reserve of combat-ready troops, able to be inserted wherever they were needed most. The problem with them lay further up the command chain. Senior Allied officers and planners still lacked the experience needed to make the most of this useful airborne asset, and found it difficult to understand that these valuable troops lacked the artillery and anti-tank resources available to 'leg infantry' divisions. Therefore, if used wisely they would prove a boon, but if landed in enemy territory they would remain vulnerable to enemy armour until the bridgehead could be expanded to encompass their landing zones.

The British 46th (North Midland) Infantry Division was formed from Territorial Army units, and despite its name it came from Hampshire and the north-east of England as well as the East Midlands. The division participated in the Fall of France (1940) and remained in Britain until late 1942, when it was sent to Tunisia as part of the British First Army. During February and March 1943 it was involved in heavy fighting around Hunt's Gap, and suffered extensive casualties. While these losses had been replaced by

Major-General Ridgeway, commander of the US 82nd Airborne Division, receives a report from a lieutenant of the 36th Infantry Division in Altavilla shortly after the town was finally captured by Ridgeway's paratroopers.

September, many of these new troops lacked the experience of the division's surviving veteran cadre. Therefore the division can be regarded as being reliable, particularly in defence, but lacking in experience and aggression.

The British 56th Division had also played its part in the closing stages of the Tunisian Campaign, but its combat experience was minimal. Like its companion division, the 56th was composed largely of Territorial Army units and, while well enough trained, these troops were still learning what 'real soldiering' was all about. These largely raw troops would face highly

experienced German troops who were masters in the art of modern warfare. Of its two brigades, the 169th (Queens) Brigade was seen as the most reliable. Fortunately Major-General Graham had the 201st Guards Brigade attached to his division. Formerly the 22nd Guards Brigade, this brigade had spent two years fighting its way from Tobruk to Tunis with Montgomery's Eighth Army, despite losing most of its original complement at the fall of Tobruk (1941). It was both battle-hardened and experienced, but during the Salerno campaign it would be wasted in largely fruitless attacks against the 'Tobacco Factory' to the west of Battipaglia.

The US 36th Infantry Division was composed of men from the Texas National Guard who had little experience of combat. When the division landed in North Africa five months earlier its level of training was considered barely adequate, but since then the divisional commander Major-General Fred Walker had demanded that his men train hard to improve their weapons skills and combat techniques. The division was also selected for training in amphibious landing, and so it was virtually inevitable that after being left behind during the invasion of Sicily, Walker's Texans would be used to spearhead Operation *Avalanche*. By September Walker considered his men to be ready for combat. In the ensuing campaign they would fight well enough, but they lacked the slick professionalism of their German opponents.

Major-General Dawley also commanded the US 45th 'Thunderbird' Infantry Division, which had seen some action in Sicily and so was considered 'blooded'. However, during the campaign it was claimed that Major-General Troy Middleton's division lacked spirit and ability. Like the men of Dawley's other division, the men of the 45th were National Guardsmen, this time from Oklahoma, New Mexico, Arizona and Colorado. They were inadequately trained for a division about to be thrust into combat, but nevertheless these young GIs fought hard when the time came and, occasionally, their persistence in attack and doggedness in defence did them credit. Unfortunately the soldiers of both of these US infantry divisions would have to learn their job the hard way in the Tobacco Factory and the hills around Altavilla.

The British 7th Armoured Division was by far the most experienced formation in the Fifth US Army's pool of reinforcements. It had fought its way across North Africa, and, after almost three years of fighting the division was a thoroughly battle-hardened and highly experienced formation – perhaps too battle hardened. The other reinforcements – all American formations – would arrive at Salerno too late to take an active part in the campaign.

An American M1 155mm howitzer in action in defence of the American bridgehead. The howitzer belonged to the 189th Field Artillery Battalion, attached to the US 45th Infantry Division. These guns had a range of over 9 miles, but given the high angle of elevation this weapon was firing at a target less than 5 miles away.

ORDERS OF BATTLE

GERMAN ORDER OF BATTLE

AOK 10 (GEN. HEINRICH VON VIETINGHOFF)

XIV Panzer Korps (Gen. der Panzertruppen Hermann Balck)

16. Panzer-Division (Gen.Lt. Rudolph Sieckenius)

 Kampfgruppe Dörnemann (Maj. Dörnemann)

  Panzer-Aufklärungs-Abteilung 16

  One company, III/Panzer-Regiment 2

   (Stug III assault guns)

  Engineer detachment, Pionier-Bataillon 16

 Kampfgruppe von Holtey (Obst. von Holtey)

  Two companies, II/Panzer-Regiment 2 (PzKpfw IVs)

  Artillery battalion, Artillerie-Regiment 16

  Engineer detachment, Pionier-Bataillon 16

 Kampfgruppe von Doering (Obst. von Doering)

  Panzergrenadier-Regiment 79 (two battalions)

  Two companies, II/Panzer-Regiment 2 (PzKpfw IVs)

  Artillery battalion, Artillerie-Regiment 16

  Engineer detachment, Pionier-Bataillon 16

 Kampfgruppe Stempel (Obst. Stempel)

  Panzergrenadier-Regiment 64 (two battalions – one equipped with half-tracks)

  III/Panzer-Regiment 2, less one company (Stug IIIs)

  Artillery battalion, Artillerie-Regiment 16

  Engineer detachment, Pionier-Bataillon 16

Panzer-Division 'Hermann Göring' (Gen.Maj. Wilhelm Schmalz)

 Kampfgruppe Haas (Obst. Haas)

  II and III/Panzergrenadier-Regiment 115

  Panzer-Aufklärungs-Abteilung 'Hermann Göring'

  III/Panzer-Regiment 'Hermann Göring' – less one company (Stug IIIs)

  Composite battalion, Panzer-Regiment 'Hermann Göring' (mainly PzKpfw IVs)

  Artillery battalion, Artillerie-Regiment 'Hermann Göring'

  Engineer detachment, Pionier-Bataillon 'Hermann Göring'

 Kampfgruppe Becker (Maj. Becker)

  III/Fallschirmjäger-Regiment 1

15. Panzergrenadier-Division (Gen.Lt. Eberhard Rodt)

 Kampfgruppe Stroh (Obst. Stroh)

  Panzergrenadier-Regiment 129 (two battalions)

  Panzer-Abteilung 215 (mainly PzKpfw IVs)

  Werfer-Regiment 71 (Nebelwerfer mortars)

  One company, III/Panzer-Regiment 'Hermann Göring' (Stug IIIs)

  Artillery battalion, Artillerie-Regiment 15

  Engineer detachment, Pionier-Bataillon 15

LXXVI Panzer Korps (Gen. der Panzertruppen Traugott Herr)

26. Panzer-Division (Gen.Lt. Smilo Freiherr von Lüttwitz)

 Kampfgruppe (commander unknown)

  II/Panzergrenadier-Regiment 9

  I and III/Fallschirmjäger-Regiment 4

  Aufklarungs-Abteilung 129

  Artillery battalion, Artillerie-Regiment 26

  Engineer detachment, Pionier-Bataillon 15

3. Panzergrenadier-Division (Gen.Lt. Fitz-Hubert Grässer)

 Kampfgruppe Moldenhauer (Maj. Moldenhauer)

  I/Panzergrenadier-Regiment 29

  II/Panzergrenadier-Regiment 67 (attached from 26. Panzer-Division)

  Aufklarungs-Abteilung 103

  Panzer-Abteilung 103 (Stug IIIs)

29. Panzergrenadier-Division (Gen.Lt. Walter Freis)

 Kampfgruppe Ulich (Obst. Ulich)

  I and III/Panzergrenadier-Regiment 15 (I Bn. in half-tracks)

  Aufklarungs-Abteilung 26

  Engineer detachment

 Kampfgruppe Krüger (Obst.Lt. Krüger)

  Panzergrenadier-Regiment 71 (two battalions)

ALLIED ORDER OF BATTLE

FIFTH US ARMY (LT. GEN. MARK CLARK)

British Commando Brigade [attached] (Brig. Laycock)

 41 Royal Marine Commando

 No. 2 Army Commando

US Ranger Force [attached] (Col. Darby)

 1st Rangers

 2nd Rangers

 4th Rangers

US 82nd 'All American' Airborne Division (Maj. Gen. Matthew B. Ridgeway)

 319th and 320th Glider Field Artillery Battalions

 376th and 476th Parachute Field Artillery Battalions

 307th Airborne Engineer Battalion

 80th Airborne Anti-Aircraft Battalion (also included anti-tank assets)

 509th Parachute Infantry Battalion [attached] (Lt. Col. Yardley)

 504th Parachute Infantry Regiment [PIR] (Col. Tucker)

 505th Parachute Infantry Regiment (Col. Gavin)

 325th Glider Infantry Regiment (Col. Easley)

US VI Corps (Maj. Gen. Ernest J. Dawley)

191st Tank Battalion

601st and 636th Tank Destroyer Battalions

57th Signal Battalion

2nd and 83rd Chemical Mortar Battalions

US 36th 'Texas' Infantry Division (Maj. Gen. Fred L. Walker)

    141st Regimental Combat Team [RCT] (Colonel Werner)

    142nd Regimental Combat Team (Lt. Col. Forsyth)

    143rd Regimental Combat Team (Col. Martin)

    131st, 132nd and 133rd Field Artillery Battalions

    751st Medium Tank Battalion

    155th Field Engineer Battalion

    36th Divisional Signals Detachment

US 45th 'Thunderbird' Infantry Division
(Maj. Gen. Troy H. Middleton)

    157th Regimental Combat Team (Col. Ankcorn)

    179th Regimental Combat Team (Col. Hutchins)

    180th Regimental Combat Team (Col. Ryder)

    158th, 160th, 171st and 189th Field Artillery Battalions

    753rd Medium Tank Battalion

    120th Field Engineer Battalion

    45th Divisional Signals Detachment

British X Corps (Lt. Gen. Richard McCreery)

Royal Scots Greys (Sherman tanks, attached to 56th Division)

40th Royal Tank Regiment
(Shermans, attached to 46th Division)

46th (North Midland) Infantry Division
(Maj. Gen. John Hawkesworth)

    46th Reconnaissance Regiment

    2nd Battalion Northumberland Fusiliers (machine-gun battalion)

    70th, 71st and 172nd Field Regiments, Royal Artillery

    58th Anti-Tank Regiment, Royal Artillery

    5th Medium Regiment, Royal Artillery

    115th Light Anti-Aircraft Regiment, Royal Artillery

    270th, 271st and 272nd Field Companies,
    Royal Engineers

    273rd Field Park Company, Royal Engineers

    128th Infantry Brigade (Brig. James)

        1/4th Bn. Hampshire Regiment

        2nd Bn. Hampshire Regiment

        5th Bn. Hampshire Regiment

    138th Infantry Brigade (Brig. Harding)

        6th Bn. Lincolnshire Regiment

        2/4th Bn. King's Own Yorkshire Light Infantry

        6th Bn. York and Lancaster Regiment

    139th Infantry Brigade (Brig. Stott)

        2/5th Bn. Leicestershire Regiment

        5th Bn. Sherwood Foresters

        16th Bn. Durham Light Infantry

British 56th (London) Infantry Division
(Maj. Gen. Douglas Graham)

    44th Reconnaissance Regiment

    6th Bn. Cheshire Regiment (machine-gun battalion)

    64th, 65th and 113th Field Regiments, Royal Artillery

    67th Anti-Tank Regiment, Royal Artillery

    69th Medium Regiment, Royal Artillery

    57th Heavy Anti-Aircraft Regiment, Royal Artillery

    100th Light Anti-Aircraft Regiment, Royal Artillery

    220th, 221st and 42nd Field Companies, Royal
    Engineers

    563rd Field Park Company, Royal Engineers

    167th Infantry Brigade (Brig. Firth)

        8th Bn. Royal Fusiliers

        9th Bn. Royal Fusiliers

        7th Bn. Oxfordshire & Buckinghamshire
        Light Infantry

    169th Infantry Brigade (Brig. Lyne)

        2/5th Bn. Queens Regiment

        2/6th Bn. Queens Regiment

        2/7th Bn. Queens Regiment

    201st Guards Brigade (Brig. Gascoigne)

        6th Bn. Grenadier Guards

        3rd Bn. Coldstream Guards

        2nd Bn. Scots Guards

Reinforcements

US 3rd Infantry Division (Maj. Gen. Lucian Truscott)

US 34th Infantry Division (Maj. Gen. Charles W. Ryder)

US 1st Armored Division (Maj. Gen. Ernest N. Harmon)

British 7th Armoured Division (Maj. Gen. Erskine)

    11th Hussars (Reconnaissance Regiment)

    3rd, 5th Regiment, Royal Horse Artillery

    65th Anti-Tank Regiment, Royal Artillery

    15th Light Anti-Tank Regiment, Royal Artillery

    4th and 621st Field Squadrons, Royal Engineers

    143rd Field Park Squadron, Royal Engineers

    22nd Armoured Brigade (Brig. Hinde)

        1st Bn. Royal Tank Regiment (Shermans)

        5th Bn. Royal Tank Regiment (Shermans)

        4th Bn. County of London Yeomanry (Shermans)

        1st Bn. the Rifle Brigade (motorized infantry)

    131st Motorized Infantry Brigade (Brig. Whistler)

        1/5th Bn. Queen's Royal Regiment (West Surrey)

        1/6th Bn. Queen's Royal Regiment (West Surrey)

        1/7th Bn. Queen's Royal Regiment (West Surrey)

THE FLEET

TF 80 – Western Naval Task Force (Vice Admiral H. Kent Hewitt USN)

Flagship: Headquarters Ship USS *Ancon*
    (also floating HQ of General Clark)
Plus two British aircraft direction ships and three British
    hospital ships
TF 88 Support Carrier Force (Rear Admiral Sir Philip Ryan RN)
Light carrier *Unicorn*, escort carriers *Battler, Attacker, Hunter* and
    Stalker, plus light cruisers *Euryalus*, *Scylla*, *Charybdis* and
    eight destroyers.
TF 85 Northern Attack Force (Commodore Oliver RN)
    Naval Gunnery Support Group:
    Light cruisers *Mauritius*, *Uganda*, *Orion*, *Delphi*, monitor
    Roberts, plus 17 destroyers
    Transport Group (transporting British X Corps,
    Commandos and Rangers):
    Six transport ships, six LSIs
    Beach Craft Group:
    American: 45 LSTs, 24 LCts, 48 LCI(L)s
    British: 45 LSTs, 60 LCTs, 48 LCI(L)s
    Minesweeper Group: seven minesweepers,
    27 small mine craft
    Ancillary vessels: four tugs, 13 armed trawlers, 32 motor
    launches and 23 other small vessels
TF 81 Southern Attack Force (Rear Admiral John L. Hall USN)
    Fire Support Group and screen:
    Light cruisers *Philadelphia*, *Savannah*, *Boise*, *Brooklyn*,
    monitor *Abercrombie* (British), plus 16 destroyers
    Transport Group (transporting US VI corps):
    18 transport ships (six were British), three British LSTs
    Landing Craft Group:
    American: 24 LSTs, 26 LCI(L)s
    British: nine LSTs, six LCI(L)s
    Minesweeper Group: 21 minesweepers
    Ancillary vessels: two tugs, 16 PT boats, six British MTBs,
    eight patrol craft and 26 other small vessels

Covering Forces
Force 'H' (Vice Admiral Willis RN):
Battleships *Warspite* and *Valiant* plus nine destroyers
Note: battleships *Nelson* and *Rodney* were also on stand-by in
    Malta if required.
Covering Carrier Force (Rear Admiral Moody RN):
Fleet Carriers *Illustrious* and *Formidable* plus 11 destroyers
Note: These covering forces were technically independent
    of TF 80, reporting directly to Admiral Cunningham, the
    Commander-in-Chief of the Mediterranean Fleet. However,
    when they were sent to the Gulf of Salerno they were
    temporarily placed under Vice Admiral Hewitt's command.

OPPOSING PLANS

GERMAN PLANS

The Germans knew an invasion was coming – they just didn't know where. This meant that the German Armeeoberkommando (AOK) 10 – Tenth Army – had to cover against all eventualities. The XIV Panzer Korps was deployed in defence of Naples and Salerno. Of its three divisions the Panzer-Division 'Hermann Göring' was based outside Naples, while the 15. Panzergrenadier-Division covered the coastline of the Gulf of Gaeta. This left the 16. Panzer-Division deployed facing the Gulf of Salerno. If the Allies landed there then it was hoped that the other two divisions would be able to reach the area in less than a day.

To the south LXXVI Panzer Korps was deployed in Calabria and Apulia. The 29. Panzergrenadier-Division was stationed around Reggio, in the 'toe' of Italy, while the 26. Panzer-Division was stationed further inland in the mountainous region to the south of Potenza. The third division of the corps – the 1. Fallschirmjäger-Division – was deployed in Apulia, with orders to defend the ports of Bari, Brindisi and Taranto. In the event of an invasion in the south these formations would use the terrain to their advantage, delaying any attacker until reinforcements could reach them. The primary aim of the 1. Fallschirmjäger-Division though was to defend the air bases around Foggia, to the east of Naples. If attacked it would fall back towards Foggia, again making the most of the wooded, hilly terrain as it did so.

If the attack fell further north, around Naples or Salerno, then LXXVI Panzer Korps would be available to reinforce the beachhead by advancing up the road leading from Potenza to Salerno. In the event of the Allies landing in both places, then the corps commander's orders were to delay the advance of the enemy, but if possible to release whatever troops he could spare to come to the relief of XIV Panzer Korps. This centrally located Panzer corps could also expect to draw on reinforcements from the north. The XI Fliegerkorps was stationed around Rome, with the 2. Fallschirmjäger-Division based in the Frascati Hills to the south of the city, close to the beaches around Anzio, and the 3. Panzergrenadier-Division deployed close to the coastline to the north of Ostia. Although this corps was under Kesselring's direct control, it too could be sent south, to join in the fighting wherever the Allies chose to land.

Other German troops were available too, but as these were stationed in northern Italy it would take time for them to reach the invasion beaches.

The Gulf of Salerno and its environs

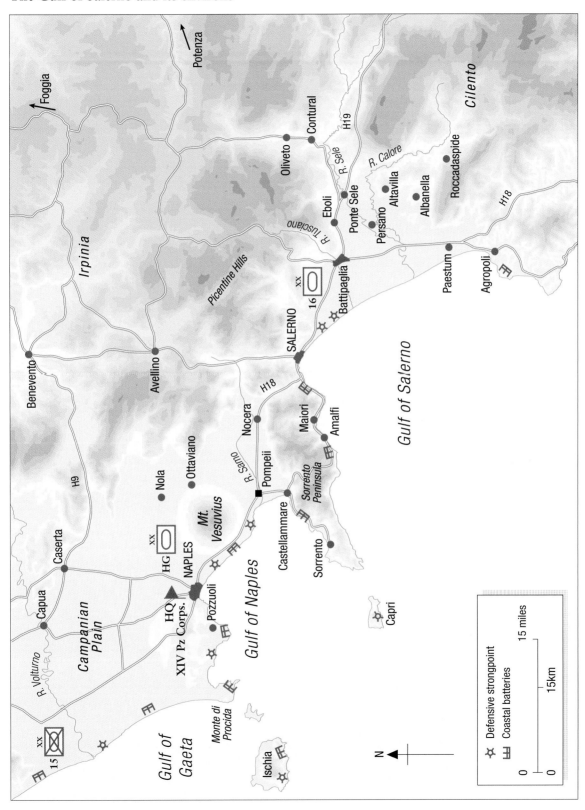

The harbour front of Salerno as it appeared during the campaign, viewed from the north side of the port below 'Monument Hill', looking towards the west. Behind the port is 'White House Hill', with Monte Monna behind it.

The German strategy was to pin the Allies in their bridgehead, and to launch a series of powerful combined arms assaults to keep them off-balance. When sufficient forces had arrived, then a major counter-attack would attempt to drive the enemy into the sea.

As most of the German units in Southern Italy were mechanized, and at least the leading waves of any landing force would be infantry, it was hoped that the Germans would be able to exploit their temporary superiority in armour before the Allies could land sufficient tanks to nullify this German advantage. Similarly, if one discounted naval gunfire support, not only would the Germans enjoy a superiority in artillery on the battlefield, but by holding the high ground beyond the beaches it was hoped that German artillery observers would be better placed to direct fire where it was needed most. Above all, the Germans hoped to take advantage of any superiority they might enjoy in troop quality and numbers during the first days of the battle. For them, success was all about reacting swiftly to the Allied landing and aggressively battering away at the beachhead before the enemy could consolidate it.

Two knocked-out German tanks from the 16. Panzer-Division, destroyed by a 6-pdr anti-tank gun belonging to the 8th Royal Fusiliers during the fighting along the river Tusciano. The tank in the foreground is a PzKpfw III equipped with a flamethrower.

ALLIED PLANS

Operation *Avalanche*, the amphibious landing at Salerno, was a large and complex operation, which tested the planning skills of the Allies to the limit. It involved the interplay of land, sea and air elements, and its success depended on a whole host of variables, from tide times and offshore currents to the range of a Spitfire with a drop tank of fuel. The planners were given an additional headache because there was a shortage of landing craft. Those used in Operation *Husky* were re-used

for *Baytown* and then *Avalanche*, and while the number available declined slightly due to combat losses and mechanical problems, at least the crews of these all-important craft were now fairly experienced, and knew what to expect. While the fighting raged in Sicily, staff in Eisenhower and Clark's headquarters laid the groundwork for the next great venture.

The Salerno plain, viewed from an American aircraft flying low over the southern outskirts of Salerno. The railway line leading to Battipaglia stretches away to the south. On the left of it are the Picenti Hills, while to the right are the British invasion beaches.

Avalanche was a daring operation, but one which could potentially reap significant rewards if it proved a success. The big prize was Naples, the most populous city in the south of Italy, and one that possessed the best port facilities on Italy's western coast, south of Genoa. The Allies needed Naples to supply their army as it advanced northwards towards Rome. Both sides understood the importance of this great port, and were prepared to fight hard for it.

Lieutenant-General Mark Clark's Fifth US Army would mount the operation, and D-Day was set for the early morning of 9 September. This was just three weeks after the fighting ended in Sicily, and a week after Montgomery's crossing of the Straits of Messina. Now, after weeks of fighting by the Seventh US and British Eighth Armies, it was finally Clark's turn. His army consisted of the British X Corps and the US VI Corps. Lieutenant-General Sir Richard McCreery and his British X Corps would land on the left, just below the port of Salerno. This was to be the main assault, and McCreery's immediate objectives were the mountain passes to the north, the port of Salerno itself, Montecorvino airfield and the important road and rail junction of Battipaglia.

On his left flank, on the Sorrento Peninsula, three battalions of US Rangers would land at the small port of Maiori, while two battalions of Commandos would land at Vietri, between Maiori and Salerno. The Rangers' task was to seize the Nocera Pass, and with it the main road to Naples, while the Commandos would occupy the Cava Defile, to the north-west of Salerno. If these locations could be held, then the Germans would find it difficult to reach the Salerno plain from the north. This was a vital mission, and McCreery hoped that as soon as Salerno was captured he would be able to swing at least one of his two divisions northwards, to take over control of these positions from his special forces.

The bulk of McCreery's corps would land on a 7-mile stretch of beach between the mouth of the small river Picento and the larger river Sele, which would serve as the boundary between the British and American sectors.

The 46th Division would land on the left, on a 3-mile frontage, opposite the little hamlet and enemy strongpoint known as Magazzeno. This was essentially a one-brigade frontage – subsequent waves of the division would reinforce the initial brigade-sized landing force. The beaches of the British 46th Infantry Division were code-named 'Uncle' and 'Sugar', the dividing line between them being the mouth of the small river Asa.

The southern limit of Sugar Beach was the mouth of the river Tusciano, the largest of the three small rivers which flowed into the Gulf north of the larger river Sele. Between the Tusciano and the Sele lay 'Roger' Beach. That was where the British 56th Infantry Division would land, on a two-brigade frontage. The British would benefit from a naval bombardment before the landing craft reached the beaches, and landing vessels equipped with rockets would also support them. They would saturate the area around Magazzeno just as the landing craft were making their final approach. If all went well the defenders would be too dazed to offer much resistance.

As soon as the beachhead was secured the 46th Division would advance 4 miles to Salerno, and seize the port before the Germans could bring in reinforcements. The 'stop line' for D-Day lay in the foothills to the north and west of the town. The division would also link up with the Commandos at Vietri. Meanwhile the 56th Division would advance across the Salerno plain, and seize Montecorvino airfield, which lay 2 miles inland, and the town of Battipaglia, which lay 4 miles from the coast. Their D-Day 'stop line' lay just beyond the town, in the high ground to the north.

Meanwhile, on the far side of the river Sele, Major-General Ernest J. Dawley's US VI Corps would land in front of the ruins of Paestum, on a 3-mile frontage. Due to a shortage of landing craft only one of Dawley's two divisions would land on D-Day – the other would form a floating reserve. The US 36th Infantry Division would lead the assault with two of its Regimental Combat Teams (RCTs), one landing behind the other. Their mission was to capture the high ground overlooking the Salerno plain, and to prevent German forces from entering the plain from the south and east. Once the small village and its adjacent complex of Greco-Roman ruins were secured, the 36th Division would occupy Mt Soprano to the east of the beaches, while the small river Solofrone to the south of Paestum would form the division's southern 'stop line'. To the north, the American troops would fan out to secure the crossings over the river Sele, and to be in a position to advance up the Sele Valley on D+1.

In addition, the US 82nd Airborne Division would form a strategic reserve, based in the Sicilian airfields. Within three days of the initial landing the British 7th Armoured Division, the US 3rd Infantry Division and several army and corps level assets would also be landed on the Salerno beaches, to reinforce the beachhead. By then it was hoped that the 16. Panzer-Division would have been dealt with, Dawley's corps would be occupying the mountain passes well to the south and west of the bridgehead, and McCreery's troops would be ready to begin their advance on Naples.

Although it was the largest of the 'rivers' crossing the Salerno plain, the river Sele – seen here near the Tobacco Factory – was little more than a large stream. However, it was sufficiently wide to prevent the movement of tanks and vehicles. The river was originally meant to mark the dividing line between the British and American beachheads.

The two British and two US infantry divisions that would lead the assault were scattered in various harbours throughout the Western Mediterranean. The job of Vice-Admiral Hewitt USN, commanding the Western Naval Task Force, was to escort these troops to a rendezvous off the coast of Salerno, and then to escort them safely to their designated beaches. As well as over 330 landing craft of various types, and over two dozen transport ships, Hewitt also had flotillas of minesweepers to clear the approaches, tugs and motor launches to help deal with any problems in the landing areas and even a submarine to act as a beacon, to guide his ships towards the beaches.

British Universal Carriers belonging to the 6th Lincolnshire Regiment of the British 46th Division disembarking from an American LST on Uncle Red Beach. The sea in the background looks deceptively empty, as this photograph was taken on the extreme left edge of the British beaches.

His force was protected by two groups of warships – the Northern (British) and Southern Attack (US) Forces, which consisted of light cruisers and destroyers to provide naval gunfire support. Rear-Admiral Vian's Support Covering Force of five small British carriers was on hand to provide air cover for the fleet. Hewitt could also draw on support from the British fleet carriers *Illustrious* and *Formidable*, and the battleships *Warspite* and *Valiant*. This gave the Allies a formidable level of firepower, but this large fleet concentrated in a relatively confined space was also extremely vulnerable to air attack.

Lieutenant-General Clark was optimistic. Intelligence reports told him that the only immediate threat to the landing would come from the 16. Panzer-Division, commanded by Gen.Lt. Sieckenius, which was stationed in the Salerno area. While details of its actual dispositions were hazy, reports suggested that it was still woefully under-strength after its withdrawal from Sicily and that, while it remained a potent threat, it was unlikely that it would be able to concentrate its forces before the Allies had lodged themselves on the Salerno plain. Then, a combination of naval firepower and sheer weight of numbers would serve to nullify the threat, and allow Clark to concentrate on his advance on Naples.

During the days preceding the invasion, four large convoys set out from four North African and Sicilian ports. The British 46th Division sailed from Bizerte in Tunisia, while the British 56th Division sailed from Tripoli. The US 36th Division embarked in Oran in Algeria, and the US 45th Division, fresh from the Sicilian campaign, set sail from Palermo on the north coast of Sicily. These four groups all rendezvoused in the Tyrrhenian Sea on 8 September, and together the great invasion fleet set a course for the Gulf of Salerno. While every effort was made to keep the enterprise a secret, German aircraft spotted the ships as they rounded the western tip of Sicily. Still, it was hoped that while the Germans might know they were coming, they still remained unsure exactly where the armada was bound. Others though, were quite certain. The writer Erik Linklater was on a troopship that sailed out of Tripoli on 6 September. As they slipped out of the harbour the Chinese cook on a water boat shouted out 'See you in Naples!' The big question was – would the Germans be as well informed as the Chinese cook?

OPERATION *AVALANCHE*

The very nature of amphibious invasions is that, at least in theory, the attacker can choose the battlefield, and should be able to catch the defenders largely unaware. Neither of these advantages really applied at Salerno – the Germans knew that an invasion force was coming, the only question was where the landing would come. Kesselring and his senior officers had to cover all eventualities, but the balance of probability suggested that the Allies would land somewhere near Naples. Coastal defences in the area were in Italian hands, leaving the Germans able to hold themselves in readiness for a powerful counter-attack. However, on the evening of 8 September news of the Italian surrender was announced by General Eisenhower, and was deemed to be effective immediately. The Italian government had been forced to play its hand, and in response the Germans launched Operation *Axis*, the military seizure of Italy. This involved disarming Italian units, taking over Italian positions and capturing the Italian navy. In the Salerno area, units of the 16. Panzer-Division and other formations assumed control of the Italian coastal batteries on the Amalfi coast, as well as the beach defences in Paestum and Magazzeno. By 0200hrs at the latest these positions were manned and ready.

The long, narrow beach running from Salerno to Paestum was empty of the landing obstacles used in Normandy. However, parts of the area immediately behind the beach were mined, while observation points and strongpoints were sited so that the defenders could harass and slow down any landing. Artillery batteries deployed in the foothills behind the Salerno plain could therefore bring down accurate fire on the attackers, while the same high ground could be used to keep the Allies under observation and artillery fire as they moved inland. The beachhead was divided by several small rivers, none of which posed a major obstacle, but which would serve to channel any

British infantry and vehicles being unloaded on Uncle Beach from LST-383, a US tank landing ship, partly obscured in the smoke from other burning vessels. Other troops ferry supplies from the vessel under the watchful eye of a beachmaster.

advance from the beach. The Salerno plain itself was dotted with small farms, irrigation ditches, thickets of rushes, orchards and small groves, all of which provided good cover for the German defenders. Then, behind the beaches, the main road – Highway 18 – proved an excellent conduit for German reinforcements, and allowed them to move units freely to meet any Allied threat. Clearly cutting this road would be a major objective for the Allies on D-Day.

By 0130hrs the great Allied armada had entered the Gulf of Salerno, and was welcomed by fire from coastal batteries sited along the Amalfi Coast. These were soon silenced by naval gunnery, and the invasion fleet continued on its way. At 0200hrs the Northern and Southern Task Forces separated, as each headed towards their designated beaches. The covering force of light carriers took up station further out to sea, ready to provide air cover for the invasion fleet while it unloaded its human cargo. An hour later, at 0300hrs, the transports reached their designated areas, and the troops began clambering from the big transport ships into their smaller landing craft. The invasion was now under way.

A US Ranger patrol in action near the Chiunzi Pass. Aggressive patrolling by Darby's Rangers did much to discomfit Panzer-Division 'Hermann Göring' during the battle, and helped prevent the development of a large-scale German attack against the Maiori beachhead.

THE LANDINGS

The first landings were scheduled to take place at 0320hrs on the left flank of the invasion beaches. On the Amalfi Coast the US Rangers were to land at the small fishing harbour of Maiori, while the British Commandos headed to Vietri a few miles to the east. The Rangers landed on schedule, wading ashore on the small beach in front of Maiori. The 4th Ranger Battalion formed the first wave, and soon discovered that there was no enemy garrison in the village. They fanned out through Maiori, and secured the beachhead before Col. Darby arrived with the remaining two battalions.

Once ashore the Rangers seized the high ground overlooking Maiori and Minori to the west, while patrols set out along the roads leading north and east. Their only casualty came when a patrol approached the lighthouse at Capo d'Orso, 2½ miles to the east, and were fired upon by its German occupants. With his landing site secure, Darby gave the order to press on inland towards his main D-Day objective – the Chiunzi Pass. The Rangers covered the 6 miles to their objective without incident, and by 0800hrs the high ground overlooking the pass had been seized, and the 1st and 3rd Ranger Battalions were digging in. The 2nd Ranger Battalion remained as a reserve in Maiori, but sent patrols along the coast to the east and west. At 1000hrs they met Commando patrols on the Vietri road, and so contact was established between the two groups of Special Forces.

A British 20mm Bofors anti-aircraft gun of the 100th Light Anti-Aircraft Regiment is landed on Sugar Amber Beach on the early morning of D-Day, while offshore a number of landing ships await their turn to unload their cargo. This regiment formed part of the 46th Division.

Five miles down the coast at Vietri the Commandos were having a tougher time of it. A German garrison held the small port, and a hidden coastal battery fired on the landing craft as they made their final approach. Naval guns soon silenced the German guns, and destroyers continued firing to pin down the garrison as the Commandos waded ashore. No. 2 (Army) Commando spearheaded the assault, and while one troop climbed the hill to attack the battery, the rest of the Commandos secured the beach, and entered Vietri. The small German garrison was soon driven off after a brief fight in the streets, but as the second wave – 41 RM (Royal Marine) Commando – began landing, the Germans shelled the beach, causing a few casualties before the Commandos could reach the cover of the village. With Vietri secured, Col. Churchill of No. 2 Commando set up an ambush position facing Salerno, while 41 RM Commando moved northwards towards Dragonea. It was now around 0430hrs, and to the south other British and American troops were now in action.

The British X Corps landed on three sites to the south of Salerno, designated Uncle, Sugar and Roger Beaches. On the left the 46th Division landed on Uncle Beach opposite Magazenno, with the 128th Brigade forming the first wave and the 138th Brigade following behind it. On their right the 169th Brigade of 56th Division landed on Sugar Beach, while to the right of them the 167th Brigade would come ashore on Roger Beach. The 139th Brigade of 46th Division and the 201st Guards Brigade of 56th Division remained on the transports as the floating reserve.

As the Rangers and Commandos went ashore on the Amalfi Coast the landing craft began their final approach, covered by a heavy bombardment of the beaches and their hinterland. The Germans had taken over the former Italian strongpoint near Magazenno which they code-named 'Lilienthal', and a smaller strongpoint code-named 'Moltke' a mile to the north near the mouth of the small river Picento. At 0330hrs, after 15 minutes of

British X Corps area of operations

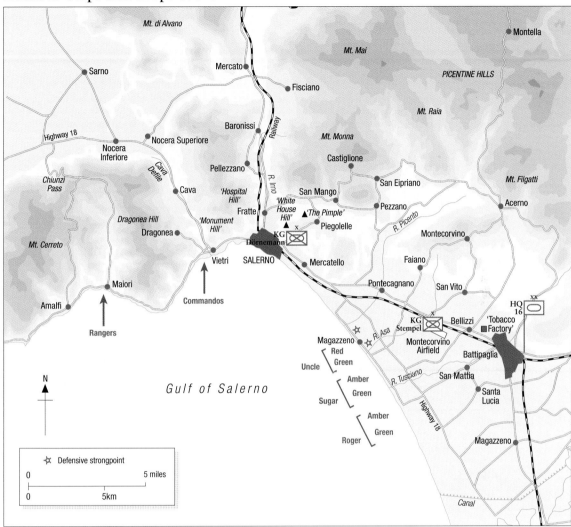

bombardment, the naval guns ceased fire and the two strongpoints were then hit by a wave of hundreds of 5in. rockets fired from specially converted tank landing craft designated Landing Craft Tank (Rocket).

The 128th Brigade was ordered to land behind the rocket barrage, and the first landing craft carrying the 1/4th Hampshires touched the beach at 0335hrs. German shells began falling from batteries sited well behind the beaches, and casualties mounted. The Germans in the two strongpoints were quick to recover from the rocket bombardment, and the intensity of enemy fire increased as the minutes passed. As engineers probed their way through suspected minefields the infantry followed behind them, eager to reach the meagre cover afforded by the beach dunes. Mines were more of a problem to the landing craft, and two LCTs were badly damaged or wrecked as they made their final approach to the beach. Others received direct hits from enemy shells.

Further to the right the 2nd Hampshires landed to the right of 'Lilienthal', but by accident they were set down on the far side of the narrow river Asa.

German prisoners being escorted to the rear by a scarf-clad British soldier – probably from No. 2 Commando. The prisoners are from Panzer-Division 'Hermann Göring', identified by their paratrooper-style camouflaged smocks.

Strangely this mistake worked in their favour, as the German defenders didn't immediately pin them down. However, they were soon being raked by machine-gun fire from 'Lilienthal'. The battalion commander ordered them to work their way up the river, to attack 'Lilienthal' from the flank. Unfortunately their support company landed on the right beach – Uncle Green – and so the rifle companies became separated from their support weapons, which meant they lacked the firepower needed to overpower the German strongpoint.

To add to the confusion the 2nd Hampshires had landed on Sugar Amber Beach, where the 2/5th Queen's Regiment of 169th Brigade were coming ashore. The result was congestion and confusion, particularly as both battalions had to wait for engineers to clear paths through the minefields in order to get off the beach. Eventually though, the troops were able to start moving. While the 2/5th Queen's engaged the defenders of 'Lilienthal' from the southern bank of the Asa, the 2nd Hampshires worked their way upstream, and crossed the small waterway to reach the back of the German position. Further south, the 2/7th Queen's landed on Sugar Green, suffering casualties from artillery as the landing craft approached the beach. Once ashore things became easier, and the battalion moved inland, where it came under fire from German machine-gun nests and snipers. By 0430hrs the 2/7th Queen's were probing their way inland towards Montecorvino airfield.

The problems encountered on Uncle Beach were repeated on Roger as the 9th Royal Fusiliers were deposited to the south of their designated landing place. They therefore became intermingled with the 8th Royal Fusiliers who were disembarking on Roger Green, and it was 0400hrs before Brig. Firth of 167th Brigade was able to restore some order, and send his men inland.

At 0530hrs when the 7th Ox and Bucks landed they were ordered to follow on behind the rest of the brigade. The first tanks of the division's attached tank regiment – the Scots Greys – joined them. By then the Londoners of Brig. Lyne's 169th Brigade were also advancing inland, the 2/7th Queen's followed by the 2/6th Queen's, who formed the brigade's second wave. So far the 56th Division was making progress – but Hawkesworth's 46th Division was still pinned down by fire from the 'Lilienthal' and 'Moltke' strongpoints.

The fleet did what it could, bringing heavy fire to bear on the German strongpoints. Meanwhile the chaos on Uncle Beach continued. Burning landing craft lit up the dawn sky, while bodies and equipment littered the narrow beach. Support weapons for the 2nd Hampshires cluttered the beach, and as their crews lacked engineering support they braved the mines to escape from the shelling on the foreshore. The chaos was heightened at 0435hrs, when the next wave landed on Uncle Green. These were the men of the 5th Hampshires, and the 2nd Hampshires should have secured their landing beach an hour before. As the first wave landed on the wrong place the 5th Hampshires found themselves exposed to fire from 'Lilienthal'. Casualties were heavy, but by 0530hrs the battalion was off the beach and skirting their way around the western end of the German defences.

By then the best part of four British battalions were firing at 'Lilienthal' and 'Moltke', and gradually the enemy fire slackened. Having held the British up for three hours, and now short of ammunition, the German defenders withdrew to the east to avoid being encircled. By 0700hrs the 128th Brigade had secured the strongpoints and was preparing to move north and east, towards Salerno and Highway 18. By then the Commandos had established themselves on Dragonea Hill and 'Monument Hill', and were sending patrols towards Cava. No. 2 Commando repulsed German probes towards Vietri from Salerno, and the expected German counter-attack never materialized. For both the Commandos and the Rangers, the afternoon of D-Day would be mercifully uneventful.

The same couldn't be said for the 128th Brigade. It began its advance from 'Lilienthal' around 0915hrs, with the 5th Hampshires leading the way. By that time the 138th Brigade were beginning to land on Uncle and Sugar Beaches, and the plan was for both brigades to advance on Pontecagnano,

In this photograph taken on one of the British landing beaches during the afternoon of D-Day a DUKW carrying ammunition comes ashore from a US LST, while the crew of a 40mm Bofors anti-aircraft gun help protect the beach from air attack.

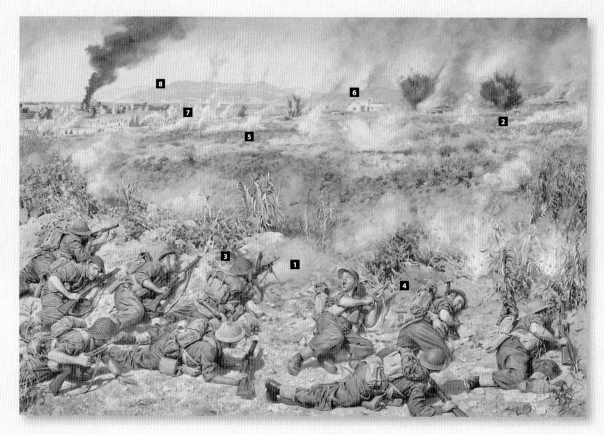

THE BATTLE FOR 'LILIENTHAL', UNCLE BEACH, 0630HRS, D-DAY (pp. 40–41)

At 0330hrs on D-Day (9 September) the German defences behind Uncle Beach were pounded by a barrage of rockets, fired from specially converted tank landing craft. This and the naval bombardment which preceded it were meant to neutralize the German strongpoint code-named 'Lilienthal' near the beachside hamlet of Magazzeno. Somehow the small German garrison survived, and as the first wave of British infantry landed the beaches were swept by machine-gun and small-arms fire. The defenders also directed the fire of German artillery onto the landing beaches. The British would be unable to expand their bridgehead until 'Lilienthal' was silenced. Although the British directly in front of this network of German positions were pinned on the beach, other battalions landing on Uncle Red or Sugar Amber Beaches managed to work their way around the flanks of the German position, while naval guns continued to bombard the defences.

'Lilienthal' consisted of several small, interlinked strongpoints – machine-gun positions, pillboxes, command bunkers and trenches, surrounded by barbed wire and mines. It had been built by the Italian army, but was now garrisoned by veteran troops from the 16. Panzer-Division. In this scene, set soon after dawn

that morning, a rifle section from the 2/5th Queen's Regiment are lining the southern bank of the small river Asa (1) little more than a stream – while machine-gun fire from a German bunker (2) sweeps the river bank. These troops have discarded their lifejackets on Sugar Amber Beach, but still retain their packs and personal equipment. A Bren gunner (3) tries to return fire, while a corporal armed with a Thompson SMG (4) encourages the rest of his section to keep their heads down. Beyond the small river lies a minefield, then a double belt of barbed wire (5). This effectively prevents any direct assault over the open ground in front of the British squad. Beyond this the German positions are being shelled by naval guns. Beyond them stands the hamlet of Magazzeno (6), while to the left waves of support troops scramble ashore onto Uncle Green Beach (7), and seek cover in the dunes. Behind them a LST is burning after receiving a direct hit from a German shell. In the distance dawn has revealed the silhouette of the Amalfi coast (8). By 0645hrs German fire had slackened, and by 0700hrs the German defenders had withdrawn inland to avoid encirclement, leaving the British 46th Infantry Division to consolidate their hold over the beachhead.

and then split up with one brigade heading for Salerno, and the other into the foothills beyond Highway 18. By 0945hrs the 5th Hampshires were advancing along a road that led east from Magazzeno towards Pontecagnano, which was lined by stone walls, and flanked by open fields. C Company was in the lead, and was only 650 yards from 'Lilienthal' when they encountered the enemy coming the other way. Three Stug III assault guns drove down the road, while Hanomag half-tracks filled with Panzergrenadiers approached through the fields on either side. With their anti-tank guns back on the beach the Hampshires were helpless. C Company and most of the battalion headquarters were virtually wiped out, while the support company in the lane behind them formed a defensive line.

The Germans worked their way around the 5th Hampshire's left flank, forcing the remaining rifle companies to withdraw back towards Magazenno. The German counter-attack was finally halted by naval gunfire, but it was now clear that the 46th Division wasn't going to advance any further that day. Instead, Hawkesworth landed his reserve brigade and formed a tight defensive perimeter, with his left flank resting on the small river Picento, his right flank on the river Asa and his front spanning what was soon dubbed 'Hampshire Lane'.

The 56th Division was having more luck. The 169th Brigade advanced across the Salerno Plain between the Asa and the Tusciano, harried by enemy snipers as they probed their way forwards. On their right the 167th Brigade encountered pockets of German resistance as it advanced. Enemy tanks held up the 8th Fusiliers west of Santa Lucia, but the 9th Fusiliers followed the southern bank of the river Tusciano to reach the outskirts of Battipaglia without much opposition.

Brigadier Firth fed his reserves – the 7th Ox and Bucks – into the fight outside Santa Lucia, but until A Squadron of the Scots Greys appeared his men lacked the anti-tank guns they needed to take on the small pockets of German armour that barred their way. For their part the Germans showed little enthusiasm to launch a determined counter-attack, as they lacked the numbers to do more than hold their ground. Still, while the 8th Fusiliers had reached Battipaglia and were fighting in its streets, the rest of Firth's brigade was unable to move up to support them before nightfall. For the moment, the 8th Fusiliers were on their own.

A patrol from the 2/5th Queens Regiment advancing through vineyards near Montecorvino Airfield. Much of the battlefield fought over by the British 56th Infantry Division was farmland, broken up by vineyards, orchards, irrigation ditches and tree-lined streams.

To the north of the Tusciano the 169th Brigade reached the southern perimeter of the airfield at around 1120hrs. The leading battalion – 2/6th Queen's – had been joined by part of C Squadron of the Scots Greys and a battery of self-propelled guns. They caused pandemonium as they swept through the boundary fence, and soon the Shermans were charging down the runway, shooting up parked and taxiing aircraft as they went. In 15 minutes, 39 German aircraft were destroyed, as well as two enemy AFVs. The Germans still held the buildings in the airfield's north-east corner, while other Germans lined the railway embankment just beyond the airfield's northern perimeter.

As German armour and anti-tank guns swung into action the British tanks withdrew, leaving the two sides holding both ends of the airfield, separated by a killing zone of open runway. Throughout the afternoon both sides launched small attacks and counter-attacks, but this stalemate continued until nightfall. This meant that the brigade had failed in its primary D-Day objective of capturing the airfield, but a little to the north the 2/7th Queens had pushed on past the airfield to cut the Salerno–Battipaglia railway and Highway 18 to the east of Pontecagnano. By nightfall the battalion had reached Faiano, in the Picentini foothills. In the process they advanced further than any other British unit on D-Day.

Taken overall the results of the day's fighting were disappointing for the British. X Corps had failed to take most of its objectives, and German opposition seemed tougher than anyone had expected. This was largely due to Gen.Lt. Sieckenius, whose 16. Panzer-Division bore the brunt of the British assault. One *Kampfgruppe* (battlegroup) was formed around Maj. Dörnemann of the division's reconnaissance battalion, which held Salerno and its surroundings throughout the day. To the south Obst. Sempel of Panzergrenadier-Regiment 64 commanded a second ad hoc *Kampfgruppe* formed from his own two battalions, a Panzer battalion (which was actually composed mainly of assault guns) and artillery. This was the *Kampfgruppe* responsible for holding 'Moltke' and 'Lilienthal', the counter-attack in 'Hampshire Lane' and the defence of Montecorvino airfield.

The Germans facing the Americans around Paestum were also from the 16. Panzer-Division. Oberst von Holtey of Panzer-Regiment 2 commanded a small Panzer reserve based around Persano, and during D-Day it would intervene in both the British and American sectors, halting the British advance around Santa Lucia and preventing the Americans from advancing beyond

A view of the American Green and Yellow Beaches on D-Day, photographed from a landing craft in the American second wave. The Torre di Paestum can be seen on the right, just above the beach. Smoke is being laid to aid the men of the initial landing wave.

US VI Corps area of operations

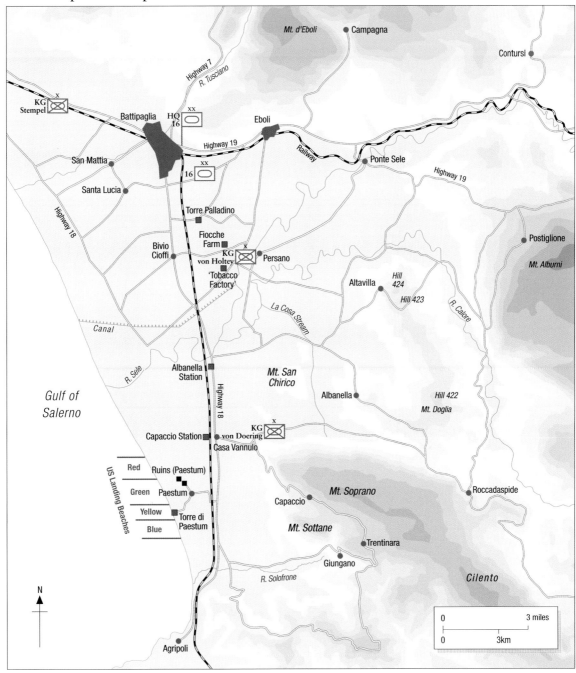

the river Sele. Then, deployed directly behind the American landing beaches was Kampfgruppe von Doering, a combined arms brigade based around Panzergrenadier-Regiment 79. During D-Day these experienced German troops would be locked in combat with the US VI Corps.

The American landing beaches stretched for 2 miles and were centred on the Greco-Roman ruins of Paestum. Major-General Dawley decided to land his leading wave without a preliminary bombardment. He counted on

By D+1 pontoon jetties had been built on both the British and American beaches, to ease the unloading of troops, vehicles and supplies. Here British infantry disembark from an American LST, while British and American engineers complete the construction of the pontoon.

speed and surprise to overpower Paestum's defenders. A lack of landing craft meant that he would attack with just one division – the Texans of the 36th Division – with two brigade-sized Regimental Combat Teams (RCTs) landing abreast of each other, while the 143rd RCT and the entire 46th Division were kept back as a reserve. The 141st RCT would land on the Yellow and Blue Beaches, to the south of Paestum, while the 142nd RCT headed towards the Red and Green Beaches, to the north of the ruins. Each regiment held one of its three battalions back as a reserve, which meant that one battalion landed on each of the four beaches.

The first wave reached the beach right on schedule at 0330hrs, but German fire proved heavy and the 142nd RCT soon found itself pinned down on the beach. To the south the 141st RCT managed to advance 430 yards before becoming pinned down by German fire. In front of Yellow beach stood the Torre di Paestum, a squat medieval tower that the Germans turned into a nest for machine-gunners and snipers. Its fire swept the entire beach, and caused havoc as the subsequent waves of landing ships arrived. On both sides of it German guns fired directly at the landing ships until they were either overrun or they withdrew. German artillery shells also fell all along the four beaches, causing mounting casualties amongst the raw Texans, many of whom lacked the experience needed to advance off the open beach.

Worse, German tanks appeared in the wood and scrub land to the south of Paestum, and by 0500hrs these had succeeded in pushing the 141st RCT back to the edge of the beach. Some of the tanks even reached the edge of the beach itself, until 1/141st RCT found itself surrounded. It was only when the reserve battalions began landing at 0530hrs that the situation improved for the Texans. The fire from the Torre di Paestum was silenced, and after a duel with support weapons deployed on the beach the German tanks withdrew inland. The 2/141st RCT fought its way through to the men of the 1st Battalion, and by 0620hrs the regiment had established itself far enough inland to protect the beaches behind them. On their left the 142nd RCT had advanced cautiously forward, clearing the scrub of German snipers as they went. By 0630hrs they were in front of the ancient walls of Paestum, which was still held by the Germans.

At 0640hrs the 143rd RCT began landing, and these fresh troops were sent forwards to Paestum after the 142nd had stormed the old outer walls, clearing it of enemy machine guns. By 0800hrs the entire complex was in American hands, and the 143rd RCT was regrouping to the east of it near Paestum station. Meanwhile, further south the Germans had launched another counter-attack against the 141st RCT, and two German tanks even broke through onto the beach, until they were driven back by fire from newly landed self-propelled howitzers and anti-aircraft guns. Eventually though, just as Paestum fell the Germans withdrew to regroup, and the Texans were able to consolidate their hold on the bridgehead.

With Paestum captured the 142nd RCT was sent off to the north, advancing up Highway 18 to seize Capaccio Station. The 141st RCT was still engaged to the south of Paestum, as the Germans continued to launch counter-attacks throughout the forenoon. Naval gunfire was instrumental in foiling these attacks, and by noon the bridgehead was deemed secure. The 143rd RCT acted as a reserve, based in Paestum. By the time 3/142nd RCT reached Capaccio Station at 1020hrs they had outpaced the rest of the regiment, and consequently were unsupported. Somehow they fought off the inevitable German counter-attack – a battalion-sized assault from Albanella Station, supported by armour. The Germans fell back to regroup, and by the time they renewed the attack at 1300hrs the 3/142nd had been reinforced, and they were driven off with relative ease.

During the afternoon the 141st RCT established a defensive line along the north bank of the river Capodefiume, while the 142nd RCT also formed a defensive perimeter around Capaccio Station. In between them the 143rd RCT was sent eastwards into the high ground overlooking the beachhead. Their objective was Monte Soprano, and by evening they had reached Hill 386, the northern spur of the mountain, and the nearby village of Capaccio. Naval gunfire was used to bombard the hill, and at 1800hrs the 3/143rd RCT assaulted it, capturing the position after a two-hour fight. Meanwhile the rest of the regiment passed through Capaccio, and reached the lower slopes of the mountain itself. They were well placed for an assault on the mountain the following morning. Once the Germans were cleared from it, their artillery observers could no longer direct fire onto the landing beaches.

All in all Dawley was pleased with progress that day. Although the 36th Division hadn't captured all of its objectives, it had established itself ashore and reinforcements could now be landed. Shermans from the 191st Tank Battalion and M10s from the 645th Tank Destroyer Battalion had reinforced the Texan infantry, and there were signs that the Germans were withdrawing from the area. In fact, Gen.Lt. Sieckenius was merely regrouping his forces, ready to renew the contest the following morning.

Gunners from the US 36th Infantry Division supervise the transport of 105mm howitzers on the landing beach at Paestum on the morning of D-Day. The guns, together with their crews and ammunition, have been loaded onto DUKWs for ease of transport across the sand.

By the afternoon of D-Day the landing beaches at Paestum were secured and the landing of troops could continue, unimpeded by German snipers and machine-gunners. However, German artillery continued to bombard the beaches throughout the day.

EXPANDING THE BRIDGEHEAD

It was a fraught night for the Allies, particularly for the British, whose bridgehead was far from secure. Still, Lt. Gen. McCreery hoped to capture Salerno the following morning, and to complete the seizure of Montecorvino airfield and Battipaglia. For their part the Germans were busy too. Generalfeldmarschall Kesselring ordered Gen. von Vietinghhoff to contest the landings, and so in turn he ordered Gen. Balck to assume control of the German forces to the north of the Allied beachhead, leaving Gen. Herr to deal with the Americans, while simultaneously slowing Gen. Montgomery's approach from the south. The longer Montgomery could be delayed the more time the Germans would have to smash the Salerno beachhead.

As 10 September dawned, the 16. Panzer-Division launched two attacks on the 9th Fusiliers in Battipaglia from two different directions. Without any anti-tank capability the outcome was never in doubt. As the morning wore on, the battalion was gradually whittled down, until by early afternoon all that was left of it was a ragged band of 200 men, led by Maj. Delaforce. They withdrew towards Santa Lucia, which the Germans had abandoned during the night, and which was now held by the 8th Fusiliers. While the garrison in the village thwarted a major German attack from the south-east, Delaforce and his men straggled back to the British lines – the last survivors of a once proud battalion.

Meanwhile, 2 miles to the north, the 201st Guards Brigade was about to go into action. It had disembarked during the night, and while the Coldstream Guards were supporting the 169th Brigade in its fight for the airfield, the Grenadiers moved north up what would become 'Grenadier Lane', which led to Highway 18 between Bellizzi and Battipaglia. In front of them lay a German-held strongpoint known as the 'Tobacco Factory', which wasn't a factory at all – just a sprawling industrial complex.[1] The guardsmen assaulted it at 0730hrs, but the attack failed, and a German counter-attack drove the Grenadiers back to their start point. The Grenadiers withdrew through their supports – the Scots Guards – who renewed the assault at 0930hrs. They too were driven back after suffering heavy casualties. They tried again that afternoon, and although the fighting lasted for the rest of the day the Scots failed to make any headway.

Two miles to the north-west the Coldstream Guards, 2/6th Queens and two squadrons of the Scots Greys resumed their attack

A British 6-pdr anti-tank gun being manhandled from a landing craft onto Sugar Beach at Salerno, while a jeep acts as its prime mover. These guns played an important role in the battle which raged for a week along the river Tusciano.

[1] To tell the two Tobacco Factories apart, the one in X Corps sector is presented in quotation marks, as it was called a 'Tobacco Factory', but was really an industrial complex. The Fiocche Tobacco Factory in VI Corps sector is simply referred to as the Tobacco Factory, with no quotation marks.

A heavily laden Universal Carrier from the Guards Brigade of the British 56th Infantry Division is pictured as it enters the ruins of Battipaglia on 18 September. Allied bombers reduced the German-held town to ruins during the days preceding the German withdrawal.

on the airfield, only to find that the Germans had abandoned it. Kampfgruppe Sempel had been recalled to Battipaglia, which Sieckenius rightly deemed to be more important than the airfield. He was already receiving reinforcements – that morning a battalion of paratroopers and a Panzergrenadier reconnaissance battalion arrived and were used to secure the German hold on the town, as well to support the first of many attacks on Santa Lucia. The result of this day of confused fighting was that the 56th Division held a line from Montecorvino to the Fosse Bridge, and maintained an increasingly well-defended forward outpost on the south bank of the Tusciano around Santa Lucia. To the south-east the 16. Panzer-Division was now concentrated around Battipaglia, with a bridgehead north of the river around the 'Tobacco Factory'. This area would form the battleground for the heavy fighting that would rage along the river Tusciano for another week.

The regrouping of the 16. Panzer-Division meant that the British 46th Division now only had Kampfgruppe Dörnemann to contend with. Patrols confirmed that the Germans had pulled back under cover of darkness, and so the 138th Brigade was ordered forwards to seize control of Salerno. They entered the town, which was gradually cleared of German snipers. Meanwhile by 1100hrs the scout cars and carriers of the 46th Reconnaissance Regiment pushed through the town to link up with the Commandos at Vietri. Brigadier Laycock's men were pleased to see them – elements of Panzer-Division 'Hermann Göring' had been gathering around Cava all morning, and were sending patrols forward to establish the extent of the Commando's positions. It was clear that an attack was imminent, but the Germans held themselves back. The same was true around the Chiunzi Pass. Although the Rangers were shelled throughout the day, no attack came. For the moment the Germans were merely testing the Allied defences.

By nightfall the British 139th Brigade had established itself around Fratte, and on 'Hospital Hill' overlooking Salerno, so named by the British because a large sanatorium dominated its summit. This meant that X Corps now held most of the Salerno Plain, including Highway 18 from Vietri to Bellizzi. Just

Note: Gridlines are shown at intervals of 1km/0.62miles

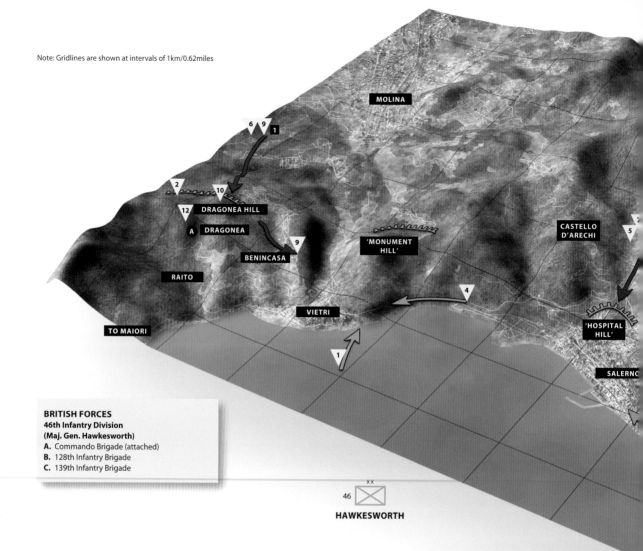

MOLINA

6 9
1

2 10

12 DRAGONEA HILL

A DRAGONEA

BENINCASA

9

RAITO

'MONUMENT HILL'

CASTELLO D'ARECHI

7
5

4

VIETRI

TO MAIORI

1

'HOSPITAL HILL'

SALERNO

BRITISH FORCES
46th Infantry Division
(Maj. Gen. Hawkesworth)
A. Commando Brigade (attached)
B. 128th Infantry Brigade
C. 139th Infantry Brigade

XX
46
HAWKESWORTH

EVENTS

Thursday 9 September (D-Day)

1. 0330hrs: Commando Brigade lands at Vietri. After clearing the town it advances to secure Dragonea Hill and 'Monument Hill'.

2. 0700hrs: Dragonea Hill occupied, while during the afternoon Commando patrols advance as far as Cava.

Friday 10 September (D+1)

3. 0800hrs: 138th Brigade clears Salerno of German snipers and spotters, although the operation takes several hours. By 1500hrs 6th Yorks & Lancs established blocking Avellino Road. Later reinforced by rest of 138th Brigade. German spotters still occupy 'White House Hill', but withdraw during the night.

4. 1100hrs: 46th Reconnaissance Regiment establishes contact with the Commando Brigade at Vietri and Dragonea.

Saturday 11 September (D+2)

5. 1210hrs: a reinforced KG Dörnemann assaults British outposts of Durham Light Infantry on 'Hospital Hill'. Meanwhile KG Stroh attacks the rest of 139th Brigade deployed in the Arno Valley around Fratte. While 'Hospital Hill' is held, the defenders of Fratte are driven back to 'White House Hill'.

6. 1630hrs: advanced elements of Panzer-Division 'Hermann Göring' probe defences of Dragonea Hill held by 412M Commando.

Sunday 12 September (D+3)

7. 1400hrs: KG Dörnemann launches major attack on 'Hospital Hill'. Fighting continues until nightfall.

8. 1640hrs: KG Stroh attacks 139th Brigade outposts on lower slopes of 'White House Hill', but assault stopped by artillery fire. Company of the Royal Leicesters is cut off.

Monday 13 September (D+4)

9. 0630hrs: KG Fritz of Panzer-Division 'Hermann Göring' attacks Dragonea Hill, supported by artillery fire. Defenders driven back as far as Vietri, but line re-formed on northern outskirts of town, and by 1200hrs the Germans forced to withdraw.

10. 1300hrs: Commando Brigade launches counter-attack. Dragonea Hill recaptured by 1430hrs.

Tuesday 14th September (D+5)

11. 0030hrs: 128th Brigade dug in on 'White House Hill' bombarded and then assaulted by KG Stroh. The 4th Hampshires' position overrun. By 1020hrs the hill is in German hands, although the 5th Hampshires still retain a small foothold on its western slopes. German spotters now overlook the beachhead.

12. 1720hrs: Commando Brigade deployed at Dragonea is relieved by the 138th Brigade, and sent to Mercatello where it forms a reserve.

Wednesday 15 September (D+6)

13. 0815hrs: KG Stroh drives 5th Hampshires from foothold on 'White House Hill'. By 1200hrs the Germans have captured Piegollele and 'Commando Hill'.

14. 1145hrs: KG Moldenhauer launches determined assault on 'Hospital Hill', but is repulsed.

15. 1740hrs: Commando Brigade ordered north to recapture Piegollele and 'Commando Hill' (AKA 'The Crag'). Assault begins at 1930hrs and objectives captured. Commandos continue on to 'The Pimple', but ordered to retire at 0000hrs when, due to confusion, the 169th Brigade fails to arrive to take over their positions, the Germans re-occupy 'The Pimple' and Peigolelle.

Thursday 16 September (D+7)

16. 1500hrs: KG Stroh assaults 'Commando Hill', but is repulsed.

Friday 17 September (D+8)

17. 0210hrs: Commando Brigade clears Germans from Piegollele, but suffers heavy casualties.

18. 0430hrs: Commandos recapture 'The Pimple', but at 1100hrs KG Stroh counterattacks and defenders forced from their positions and are driven back to Piegollele. This was the last major action of the battle, as the Germans withdrew during the night of 17–18 September.

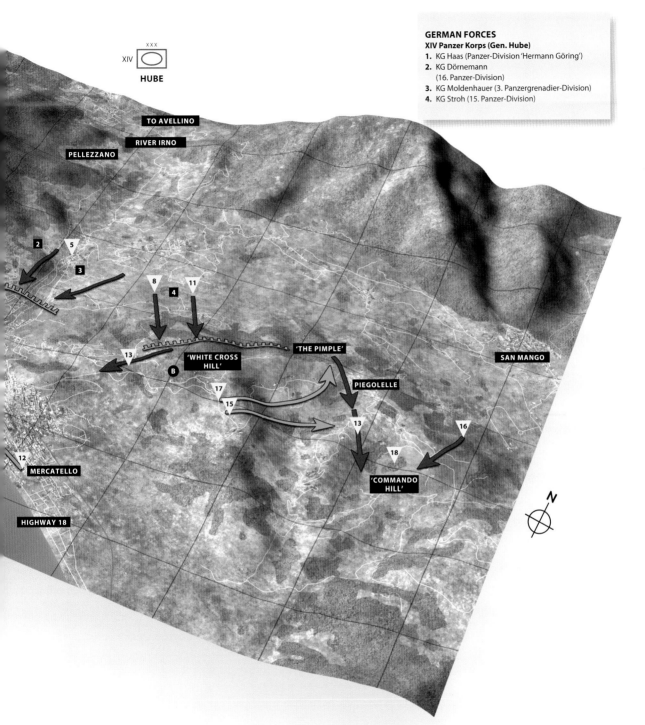

GERMAN FORCES
XIV Panzer Korps (Gen. Hube)
1. KG Haas (Panzer-Division 'Hermann Göring')
2. KG Dörnemann
   (16. Panzer-Division)
3. KG Moldenhauer (3. Panzergrenadier-Division)
4. KG Stroh (15. Panzer-Division)

XIV | HUBE

TO AVELLINO

RIVER IRNO

PELLEZZANO

2

5

3

8

4

11

13

'WHITE CROSS HILL'

B

'THE PIMPLE'

SAN MANGO

17

PIEGOLELLE

15

13

16

12

MERCATELLO

18

'COMMANDO HILL'

HIGHWAY 18

N

THE BRITISH LEFT FLANK, 9–16 SEPTEMBER 1943

On D-Day the British Commandos landed at Vietri, to protect the left flank of the beachhead. Major-General Hawkesworth's 46th Division were expected to capture Salerno on D-Day, and then advance northwards top secure the Cava Defile and the road leading towards Avellino. Instead the German defences proved tougher than anticipated, and Hawkesworth's division only linked up with the Commandos on D+1. By then the Germans had moved south from Naples and Avellino, and were poised to launch the first of a series of attacks against the British left flank. Rather than spearheading an advance on Naples, Hawkesworth's men found themselves fighting to defend their bridgehead.

A Sherman tank comes ashore on Paestum beach. While the initial landings included supporting tanks carried on small LCTs, this photograph was taken during the afternoon of D-Day, when the bulk of 751st Tank Battalion was landed from larger LSTs.

how fragile this perimeter was would be demonstrated the following morning when the Germans finally launched their counter-attack. There was also a 10-mile gap between the British and American bridgeheads, and while Dawley's men were close to the assigned corps boundary of the river Sele, it was clear that the British were temporarily unable to expand their bridgehead to the south.

In VI Corps' sector D+1 had also been marked by a rapid expansion of the bridgehead. The Germans had withdrawn during the night, and so Maj. Gen. Walker felt confident enough to widen his foothold. The 141st RCT was sent south to form a new defensive line along the river Solofrone, thus blocking any German assault from the south. The 142nd RCT was sent eastwards to secure Monte Soprano and to capture the villages of Albanella and Roccadapide beyond it. The 143rd RCT was held in reserve around Cappacio.

At 1140hrs that morning the first units of the 45th Division began landing on pontoons that had been built by engineers during the night. They were ordered to seize the crossings over the river Sele, and then to advance up the river valley towards Ponte Sele. However, by dusk the 179th RCT, which formed the division's spearhead, had only got as far as Albanella Station. There, engineers were still building a bridge across the river next to the one blown up by the retreating Germans. Therefore, during the evening the regiment moved up the southern bank of the river to its junction with the smaller river Calore. There yet more engineers were busy replacing another blown bridge, and so after outposts had been established on its far bank the regiment bivouacked for the night, ready to resume its advance in the morning.

That afternoon Lt. Gen. Clark landed at Paestum, and toured the American bridgehead. A PT boat then ferried him north to meet Lt. Gen. McCreery, whose headquarters had been established near Magazenno. Clark and his two corps commanders must have congratulated themselves that the day had passed without any major disaster, apart from the loss of the 9th Fusiliers and the repulse of the Guards Brigade. The Americans were advancing without encountering any serious opposition, and the harder-pressed British were also expanding their bridgehead. Reinforcements were also on their way. What Clark and his senior commanders didn't know was that the Germans were also being reinforced – and their fresh troops would be the first to arrive.

THE LEFT FLANK

When the blow came, it fell on the British troops guarding the northern approaches to Salerno. As the Allies now stood between it and his headquarters, Gen.Lt. Sieckenius relinquished control of Kampfgruppe Dörnemann to XIV Panzer Korps so he could concentrate on the battle around Battipaglia and the river Sele. The previous day Kampfgruppe Dörnemann, based at Baronissi, had been reinforced by a company of Stug III assault guns, detached from the division's Panzer-Regiment 2. This gave Maj. Dörnemann a powerful mechanized force – a reinforced battalion. During the night of 10/11 September he had also been reinforced by the reconnaissance battalion of 15. Panzer-Division.

The following morning Obst. Stroh of 15. Panzer-Division's Werfer-Regiment 71 arrived, leading another ad hoc *Kampfgruppe*. It consisted of a regiment of Panzergrenadiers, an under-strength composite battalion of 25 tanks and assault guns and Stroh's own mortar regiment. As the day wore on a battalion of artillery and a detachment of engineers would reinforce it. The addition of this mechanized brigade-sized force meant that Gen. Balck's XIV Panzer Korps now had the wherewithal to launch a counter-attack. The assault was timed to start at noon, with Dörnemann ordered to clear the British from 'Hospital Hill' while Stroh concentrated on the British in the valley of the small river Irno, who were concentrated around Fratte.

Brigadier Stott's 139th Brigade was deployed in a curved line, running from 'Hospital Hill' which was held by 16th Durham Light Infantry, then on

A British M4A3 Sherman tank belonging to the Scots Greys pictured during the fighting along the river Tusciano. The circle denotes it belongs to B Squadron, and the vehicle is painted in the light mud and blue-black colour scheme first adopted by the regiment in Tunisia.

On 10 September the British 46th Infantry Division entered Salerno, which had been abandoned by the Germans. Here men of the 6th York and Lancaster Regiment of 138th Brigade enter the town along the Via Torrione. Castle Hill can be seen in the distance.

to the bridge over the Irno at Fratte, defended by the 5th Sherwood Foresters. Stott's third battalion, the 2/5th Royal Leicesters, was echeloned behind the Foresters and slightly to the right, between Fratte and the slopes of the ridge the British dubbed 'White House Hill'. The British spent the morning of 11 September digging in, facing north. Still, Stott was well aware that his line was a weak one, as thanks to the Irno his two battalions on its eastern bank were unable to offer any support to the defenders of 'Hospital Hill'.

At noon the Germans began their assault, preceded by a short artillery bombardment around the Fratte Bridge and the forward slopes of 'Hospital Hill'. The Durhams were hard pressed, but held their positions on the northern and north-eastern sides of the hill, despite their lack of anti-tank weapons. Kampfgruppe Dörnemann was hindered by the lack of good roads in the area, and by the ability of the defenders to call down naval gunfire support. This curtain of fire proved too much for the Germans, and after an hour the assault was called off.

The attack on the Sherwood Foresters at Fratte was more vigorously pursued, and soon the defenders were driven from the bridge and forced back into the town behind it. This broke Brig. Stott's link with 'Hospital Hill', which could now only be reached after a lengthy diversion through Salerno itself. By early afternoon the Foresters were driven out of the town entirely and back through the northern outskirts of Salerno. At that point Obst. Stroh turned his attention to the Leicesters, who were located behind a large cemetery complex. During the afternoon they were gradually forced to give ground, until they found themselves pushed back to the forward slopes of White House Hill. Half of the battalion found itself cut off between the cemetery and the hill, as marauding PzKpfw IVs and Stug IIIs roamed the lower slopes of the hillside. Disaster was averted only after Maj. Gen. Hawkesworth ordered all of his divisional artillery to fire in support of the battalion, backed up by the guns of the fleet.

Of Hawkesworth's other two brigades, the 138th had moved on to Vietri, where it was supporting the Commandos, and the 128th was in reserve south of Salerno, recovering from its rough handling on D-Day. The 138th was unable to leave, as Panzer-Division 'Hermann Göring' was launching heavy probes against Dragonea Hill, and attempting to penetrate the Molina Pass, which the Commandos had dubbed 'Happy Valley'. That meant that all Hawkesworth had to hand as a reserve was the division's reconnaissance regiment, which guarded the northern part of Salerno itself. Fortunately for the British the Germans abandoned their attack to regroup and re-arm, and as dusk fell the British struggled to re-form some semblance of a line, running from 'Hospital Hill' to 'White House Hill'.

During the night of 11/12 September, Brig. Laycock's Commandos were pulled out of the line, and so they became a reserve which Hawkesworth could use if he needed them, either around Dragonea, 'Hospital Hill' or 'White House Hill'. Fortunately for the 138th Brigade Dragonea Hill was shelled heavily but the aggressive probes of the previous day weren't repeated. Four miles to the west the same pattern was repeated at the Chiunzi Pass, called 'Hellfire Pass' by the Rangers. The Americans were shelled, but again no serious attack materialized.

Kampfgruppe Dörnemann launched a second attack on 'Hospital Hill' soon after dawn, overrunning the positions held by B Company of the 16th Durham Light Infantry. The British survivors withdrew up the hill to the battalion's main line of defence, halfway up the northern slope. There the line held, but throughout the morning small groups of Panzergrenadiers infiltrated the British positions, using the scattered orchards and light woods on the hill as cover. The British were eventually forced to withdraw to the crest of the hill. Behind them the sanatorium Giovanni da Procida was deemed off-limits to the Durhams, as it was still occupied by staff and patients. However, by the early afternoon of 12 September the Germans had infiltrated the hospital complex, and the staff were busy treating the wounded of both sides.

Prisoners revealed that the Germans planned to shell the sanatorium at 1800hrs, as a prelude to another major attack. That was when the British evacuated the place, or helped carry less mobile patients into the sanatorium's underground boiler room. The bombardment was duly followed by another German assault at 2000hrs, which drove the British from the buildings. This time though the hard-pressed Durhams were reinforced by relatively fresh troops – the 2/4th King's Own Yorkshire Light Infantry (KOYLI) from Brig. Harding's 138th Brigade. While the Durhams reformed on the southern slopes of the hill below the sanatorium, the 2/4th KOYLI sent two companies forward to recover the hospital complex.

Two more companies worked their way round the left flank of the hill to reach the edge of a ridge to the west, which overlooked 'Hospital Hill'. There they were able to bring down naval gunfire which fell amongst Kampfgruppe Dörnemann's reserves on the southern slopes of the hill. The close-quarter fighting around the sanatorium continued until nightfall, when the British counter-attack was called off. This meant that as darkness fell neither side remained in full control of 'Hospital Hill'.

A British Ordnance ML 3in. mortar of the 46th Division being set up in a convenient open space on the north-eastern fringe of Salerno. The British made very good use of their artillery and mortar assets during the battle.

A mile and a half to the west the remaining two battalions of Brig. Stott's 139th Brigade were deployed on 'White House Hill', their refuge the day before from the assault by Kampfgruppe Stroh. The German assault there was renewed during the morning of the 12 September. The ridge was covered in long grass, patches of open woodland and the occasional building, and once again the Germans used the terrain to infiltrate around and behind the British positions. The British were gradually driven back up the hill, and at one point – and for the second time in two days – a company of the Leicesters found itself cut off from the rest of the brigade, on the extreme western end of the ridge. The company commander formed an all-round perimeter, and these troops grimly held their ground. Elsewhere though, the German assaults were blunted by a combination of artillery fire and dogged determination.

By the end of that Sunday – 12 September, or D+3, the British were still in control of Salerno and most of 'White House Hill', but the 139th Brigade had suffered heavy casualties and was badly shaken. Lieutenant-General McCreery's only remaining reserve consisted of the three Hampshire battalions of the 128th Brigade from Hawkesworth's 46th Division, which were in Salerno, and one battalion of the Commando brigade based around Vietri. McCreery had no idea where the next attack would come from, and so these troops were held back, ready to move wherever they were needed most – Dragonea, 'White House Hill' or further south on the river Tusciano.

In fact the next day saw something of a lull in the north, as the two German formations spent the Monday replenishing their supplies and preparing for the next round of combat. Reinforcements were also arriving, from the 3. Panzergrenadier-Division. Instead the fighting shifted to Dragonea Hill. At dawn on 13 September, Kampfgruppe Fitz of

Panzer-Division 'Hermann Göring' launched its long-awaited assault on the hill, using the early morning mist as cover. Tanks on the road below fired in support of the assault and within an hour the British defenders were driven off the hill and back into Dragonea village. The hilltop defenders were men of No. 2 Commando, who had returned to the front line when the 2/4th KOYLI was sent off to 'Hospital Hill'. The other two battalions of the 138th Brigade were too busy defending the Molina Pass to help the Commandos, who were eventually driven back to the outskirts of Vietri, accompanied by Brig. Laycock's headquarters staff.

In Vietri the Royal Marines of 41 RM Commando were able to form a defensive line and the Germans were stopped short of the fishing village. The Germans were then subjected to a furious artillery barrage and forced to withdraw. Laycock seized his chance and launched a counter-attack, covered by a smokescreen laid by a US Chemical Mortar battalion which had been landed to support the Rangers. By 1430hrs Dragonea Hill was back in British hands, but the cost had been high. Laycock had lost 120 men, almost a quarter of his remaining force.

That night McCreery decided to withdraw the Commando Brigade and place it in reserve south of Salerno, at Piegollele. He had been lucky. With the exception of the dawn assault on Dragonea, on Monday the 13th the bulk of the German attacks were concentrated against the American beachhead. He and his men had been granted a short reprieve. Even the Rangers at Chiunzi were spared anything other than aggressive German patrolling and heavy shelling. It was just as well. By that stage of the battle McCreery's other formation – the 56th Division – had been fighting for survival along the banks of the river Tusciano where it too was barely holding on.

This battle-damaged viaduct spans the gorge at Vietri and serves the road which runs westwards down the Amalfi coast. The photograph was taken looking east. On the far side of the bridge the road joins the main road to Salerno, while a fork to the right leads down to Vietri's waterfront.

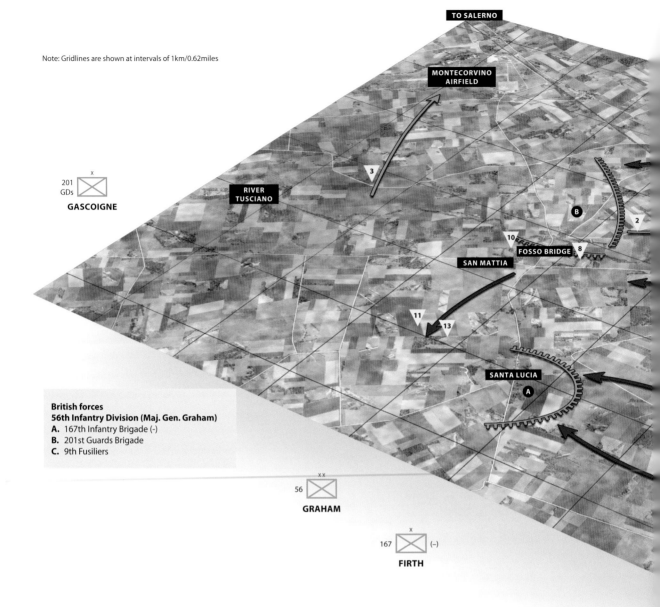

Note: Gridlines are shown at intervals of 1km/0.62miles

TO SALERNO

MONTECORVINO AIRFIELD

201 GDs
GASCOIGNE

RIVER TUSCIANO

3

B

2

10

FOSSO BRIDGE

8

SAN MATTIA

11

13

SANTA LUCIA

A

British forces
56th Infantry Division (Maj. Gen. Graham)
A. 167th Infantry Brigade (-)
B. 201st Guards Brigade
C. 9th Fusiliers

56
GRAHAM

167 (–)
FIRTH

▼ EVENTS

Friday 10 September (D+1)

1. 0700hrs: KG Stempel launches an attack on Battipaglia from the north-west. KG van Holtey launches a simultaneous attack from the south-east. 9th Fusiliers are cut off, and eventually forced to retreat. Both *Kamfgruppen* then redeploy around Battipaglia.

2. 0730hrs: Grenadier Guards advance up Grenadier Lane to bisect Highway 18, but come under heavy fire from the 'Tobacco Factory'. The attack fails. Two hours later an attack by the Scots Guards on the same German strongpoint is repulsed.

3. 0900hrs: Coldstream Guards attack in support of the 169th Brigade engaged around Montecorvino Airfield, but discover the Germans have withdrawn.

4. 1500hrs: remnants of the 9th Fusiliers make a forlorn 'last stand' south of Battipaglia. To the south, the 8th Fusiliers repulse German attack on Santa Lucia. Attacks on the hamlet from the north and west continued until nightfall.

Saturday 11 September (D+2)

5. 1400hrs: attack on Santa Lucia by KG von Doering is repulsed by British garrison, assisted by divisional artillery and naval gunfire support. A second attack launched at 1600hrs is also repulsed.

6. 1530hrs: German assault on 8th Fusiliers deployed along railway line south-west of Battipaglia. The battalion breaks, forcing Maj. Gen. Graham to rush reserves to defend Fosso Bridge supported by massed artillery.

7. 2130hrs: Scots Guards launch second attack on 'Tobacco Factory', but are repulsed with heavy losses.

Sunday 12 September (D+3)

8. 2000hrs: Germans attack British line near Fosso Bridge as remnants of 8th Fusiliers are withdrawn to beachhead. Germans eventually halted short of bridge by massed artillery barrage. That night British defences augmented by mines and barbed wire brought up from beachhead.

Monday 13 September (D+4)

9. 1500hrs: concentrated German attack down both banks of river Tusciano. Scots Guards hold line south of Bellizzi and around 'Grenadier Lane' despite casualties.

To east, Germans penetrate as far as San Mattia, which is captured at 1900hrs.

10. 2000hrs: German assault on Fosso Bridge repulsed by Scots Greys, Coldstream Guards and massed artillery.

Tuesday 14 September (D+5)

11. 1000hrs: German assault southwards from San Mattia repulsed by Scots Greys laagered south of Santa Lucia.

12. 1700hrs: third attack by Scots Guards on 'Tobacco Factory' repulsed with heavy casualties.

Wednesday 15 September (D+6)

No major fighting in sector, but British 56th Infantry Division reinforced by British armour.

Thursday 16 September (D+7)

13. 0430hrs: during night, KG Krüger infiltrated British defences around San Mattia. Dawn attack is repulsed after three hours of fighting with elements of the 201st Guards Brigade. Unsupported armoured counter-attack by Scots Greys reaches outskirts of Battipaglia before being repulsed by German anti-tank guns. This was the last German assault of the battle.

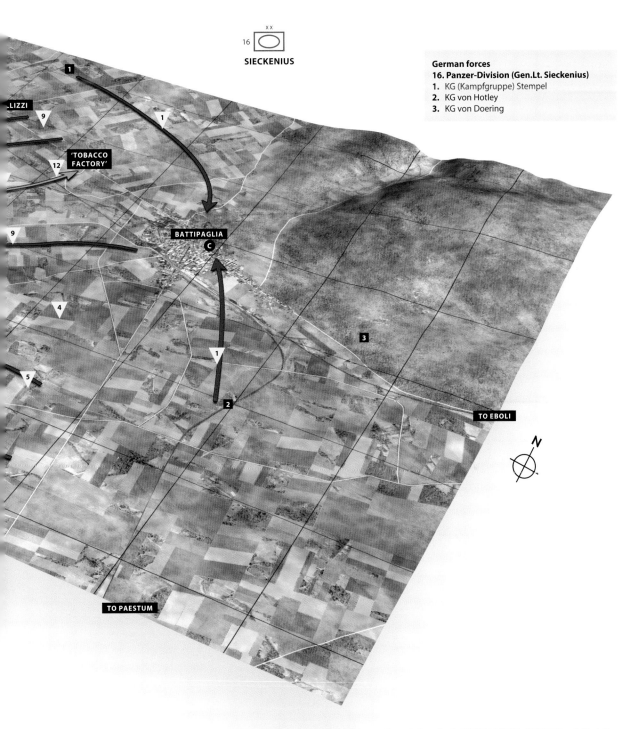

XX
16 ⬭
SIECKENIUS

German forces
16. Panzer-Division (Gen.Lt. Sieckenius)
1. KG (Kampfgruppe) Stempel
2. KG von Hotley
3. KG von Doering

LIZZI

'TOBACCO FACTORY'

BATTIPAGLIA

TO EBOLI

TO PAESTUM

N

THE RIVER TUSCIANO, 10–16 SEPTEMBER 1943

By dawn on D+1 the bulk of the British 56th Division was deployed a few miles inland from the invasion beaches, with its right flank resting on the river Tusciano, and one battalion in Battipaglia. Major-General Graham hoped to reinforce his battalion in the town during the morning. Instead the Germans struck first, initiating the first in a series of determined assaults against the right flank of the British bridgehead. For a week heavy fighting would rage along the banks of the small Italian river.

BATTLE ALONG THE TUSCIANO

While the British 46th Division was being tested in the hills north of Salerno, the men of the 56th Division were having an equally tough time of it in the southern part of the British bridgehead, along the river Tusciano. On 10 September – D+1 – the division had fought a see-saw battle in the area. It had been ejected from Battipaglia, but had captured Montecorvino airfield and advanced as far as Faiano. The Guards Brigade's assault on the 'Tobacco Factory' had been repulsed, but the 8th Fusiliers around Santa Lucia to the south of the Tusciano had held its ground in the face of fierce German attacks. The gains and losses that day had established the battle lines for the coming fight.

On the British side the 169th Brigade was spread out between Montecorvino airfield and Faiano 3 miles away to the north, while the 167th Brigade, having lost the 9th Fusiliers, was deployed in defence of the Fosso Bridge across the Tusciano, at Santa Lucia and around the bridge itself. The 201st Guards Brigade was holding the line between the airfield and the river, facing the German garrison in the 'Tobacco Factory' between Bellizzi and Battipaglia. Facing them was the 16. Panzer-Division, which was deployed between the 'Tobacco Factory' and Eboli, with the bulk of its forces grouped around Battipaglia.

That Saturday (11 September), Maj. Gen. Graham had hoped to capture the 'Tobacco Factory', and to drive the Germans beyond mortar range of Montecorvino airfield – a distance of 1½ miles. Given the resources at his disposal this seemed eminently possible as long as the Germans didn't launch an attack anywhere else. While the 169th Brigade made good progress into the foothills beyond Highway 18, the Germans proved less than obliging everywhere else on the battlefield.

Things began to go wrong in the early afternoon when Kampfgruppe von Doering launched an attack against Santa Lucia. While Kampfgruppe Krüger guarded Obst. von Doering's right flank from any intervention from the Americans, the rest of his force circled around Santa Lucia to attack the British-held village from the east. The attack was timed to begin at 1400hrs to coincide with another assault southwards from Battipaglia

Soldiers of the Royal Fusiliers manning an observation post in a ruined building on the outskirts of Battipaglia. The 9th Fusiliers were ejected from the town on D+1, and it remained in German hands throughout the rest of the battle.

by Kampfgruppe Sempel. Santa Lucia was defended by the 7th Ox and Bucks, augmented by what remained of the 9th Fusiliers. The defenders were greatly assisted by the gunners of the divisional artillery, as well as by naval gunnery. A curtain of shellfire from Graham's three regiments of 25-pdr guns prevented Doering's men from approaching the village, and so that assault was called off. Doering tried two hours later, at 1600hrs, but again concentrated British artillery fire prevented him from reaching his objective.

Kampfgruppe Sempel had more success directly south of Battipaglia. His force – II/Panzergrenadier-Regiment 64 and a battalion of PzKpfw IV tanks from Panzer-Regiment 2. The attack here was preceded by a short but concentrated artillery barrage, which fell on the 8th Fusiliers lining the railway line to the south of Battipaglia. They held on for almost two hours, but without anti-tank guns or tank support they were outgunned and outmanoeuvred. Eventually, the battalion broke and ran, heading back down the road leading to Santa Mattia and the Fosse Bridge. German tanks and half-tracks pursued them, and many of the fleeing British soldiers were cut down before they could escape.

This disaster meant that the way to the Fosse Bridge was now clear. If the Germans captured it then the garrison at Santa Lucia would be completely cut off. What saved the British was the speedy second repulse of Kampfgruppe von Doering to the east of the village. That allowed Maj. Gen. Graham to use his artillery to lay down fire on the southern approaches to the bridge. The other minor miracle for the British was that Kampfgruppe Sempel didn't have orders to capture the bridge. Having failed to break through in time to support the attack by Kampfgruppe von Doering, they were content to roam the area between Santa Mattia and the outskirts of Santa Lucia, mopping up after their victory.

The crew of a British 6-pdr anti-tank gun belonging to the Coldstream Guards guarding the northern bank of the tiny river Tusciano near the Fosse Bridge. A knocked-out German Sdkfz 251 half-track can be seen in the background.

Graham scrambled to send troops to the bridge. First to arrive was A Squadron of the Scots Greys, who had been held in reserve near Montecorvino airfield for most of the day. Next to appear was the 67th Anti-Tank Regiment, whose guns included some powerful 17-pdrs. Graham even ordered a liaison unit of US engineers, who were busy assessing the damage to Montecorvino airfield, to the scene. Reluctant to take orders from the British, they were forced to do so at gunpoint.

The German armour withdrew to Battipaglia at nightfall as Sieckenius needed to husband his resources. The Panzergrenadiers accompanied them, and so the British reoccupied the lost ground during the night. The remnants of the 8th and 9th Fusiliers were formed into a composite force, and sent to re-establish the link between the Fosse Bridge and Santa Maria. This time mines were provided to protect their front, anti-tank guns were sited and the tanks of the Scots Greys were laagered north of Santa Lucia so they could intervene if the Germans attacked again the following morning.

Strangely, when Sunday morning dawned, the anticipated German attack never came. However, as the day wore on, German reconnaissance probes against the bridgehead south of the Tusciano became increasingly aggressive. By going over to the defensive Graham had admitted that he had little chance of advancing on Battipaglia until he received reinforcements. The 167th Brigade had been bled dry, while the Guards Brigade was locked in its own deadly battle to the north at the 'Tobacco Factory'. Therefore, he decided to pull the Fusiliers back a mile, to a less exposed position closer to the bridge.

The Fusiliers began their withdrawal late that afternoon, with the support weapons withdrawing first, followed by the riflemen. Inevitably this coincided with another assault by Kampfgruppe Sempel. It was launched at 2000hrs, just as the Fusiliers were withdrawing, and for a time it looked as if the rout of the previous day would be repeated. In a repeat of the previous day's engagement a wall of shellfire halted the Germans, and eventually they pulled back. That night Graham sent the shattered 8th Fusiliers back to the bridgehead, leaving what little remained of the 9th Fusiliers to hold the line. Once again, to bolster them, anti-tank guns were sited, and mines and barbed wire were brought from the transport ships and laid in front of their positions.

Just 1½ miles away to the north-west another struggle had been raging, fought out between elements of the Guards Brigade and part of the 16. Panzer-Division. Major-General Graham saw the 'Tobacco Factory' between Bellizzi and Battipaglia as the key to the area's defences. It gave the Germans a useful lodgement on the north bank of the Tusciano – one that could be used as a springboard for a major counter-attack against the British bridgehead. Consequently, on 11 September he ordered Brig. Gascoigne's guardsmen to capture it. The Scots Guards had already assaulted the German strongpoint twice, and the Grenadier Guards had also suffered a repulse. This time the guardsmen were better prepared.

The assault went in at 2130hrs, just as that day's crisis on the far bank of the Tusciano was reaching its climax. The Scots Guards were allocated artillery support, but they still had the problem of the open ground north of the railway line. The dusk attack was designed to help, and the guardsmen moved forward behind an artillery barrage. They were also covered slightly by smoke from a burning farm silo over to their left, on the outskirts of Bellizzi. They were still met by a hail of machine-gun fire, and then subjected to a German counter-attack from their right flank – an assault supported by armour. The Scots Guards' attack ground to a halt, and worse, C Company on the right was surrounded by Germans moving up from Battipaglia. All attempts to rescue them were thwarted, and that evening the company was forced to surrender. During the attack the battalion had lost over a third of its rifle strength.

The Guards Brigade remained on the defensive the following day, as Graham might need them to intervene in the fighting for the Fosso Bridge. When this latest crisis passed Gascoigne began planning another attack – his brigade's fifth assault on the German stronghold. Instead, it was the Germans who struck first. The morning and early afternoon of 13 September had passed relatively uneventfully along the Tusciano, but it was clear to the British that the Germans were planning something. They had spent the morning probing the defences of the 169th Brigade around Faiano, but this was merely a diversion to cover the build-up of forces around Battipaglia.

A heavily laden M4A3 Sherman tank advancing from the British beachhead towards the Fosso Bridge. The censor has obliterated its unit markings, but the tank belongs to the Scots Greys. Behind it a barrage balloon can be seen, presumably tethered to a landing ship.

The main German attack was also something of a diversion, designed to pin the British in place so they wouldn't be able to intervene during the main assault, which was directed against the US VI Corps. Once again the German attack was carried out by Kampfgruppe Sempel, whose forces were divided in two. One battalion of Panzergrenadiers and a company of tanks or assault guns would advance down either bank of the river Tusciano, using the Highway 18 bridge over the river as its starting point. German artillery fired barrages in support of the attack, and Sieckenius had a reserve – a battalion of Fallschirmjäger-Regiment 1 held in readiness to exploit any success. Their objective was the Fosso Bridge.

On their right, I/Panzergrenadier-Regiment 64 approached 'Grenadier Lane', where the Scots Guards doggedly held their positions throughout the afternoon and evening. The Scots Guards had been about to launch their own attack – another attempt to capture the 'Tobacco Factory', so they were fully ready for action when the Germans launched their assault. The Grenadiers were over to the left, around Bellizzi, but the firm stand taken by the Scots Guards allowed Brig. Gascoigne to send his only reserve – the Coldstream Guards – over to the right to protect the Fosso Bridge. By nightfall on the 13th the German attack on that bank of the river had petered out.

The attack launched on the southern bank was more successful, largely because the 167th Brigade was stretched so thinly that Brig. Firth had been unable to relieve the 9th Fusiliers, who were now below half strength.

A British PIAT team pose for the cameraman, during the Salerno battle. The weapon had just been introduced into service, and the men of X Corps hadn't used it in action before the landings. This spring-loaded hollow-charge anti-tank weapon had an effective range of just over 100 yards.

Still, the battalion gave ground reluctantly, and a combination of their fire and the minefields sown in front of them resulted in mounting casualties for II/Panzergrenadier-Regiment 64. However, the British line was thinly held, and at 1640hrs Sempel ordered the paratroopers forward, who infiltrated the Fusiliers' line. By 1730hrs these fresh German troops had fought their way through to the hamlet of San Mattia, which they secured. What was left of the Fusiliers withdrew to the bridge, which B Squadron of the Scots Greys crossed at 1700hrs and established a cordon around. When the Coldstream Guards moved up to support them the immediate threat to the bridge receded.

The following morning – Tuesday 14 September – the German paratroopers at San Mattia resumed their advance, this time heading towards the sea and Roger Beach. The Panzergrenadiers of II/Panzergrenadier-Regiment 64 also tested the defences of the Fosso Bridge, but the British cordon there held. In fact, the Germans decided the bridge was now too well defended to capture by anything other than a full-scale assault. To the west of San Mattia, A Squadron of the Scots Greys thwarted all German attempts to advance closer to the beaches, supported by naval gunnery. By mid-afternoon the paratroopers had been recalled from San Mattia, and the now badly battered Kampfgruppe Sempel withdrew slightly, moving closer to Battipaglia where it was able to reorganize itself and prepare for the next round of fighting.

Meanwhile, across the river the Scots Guards finally launched the fourth assault on the 'Tobacco Factory' at 1700hrs, an attack which had been delayed for 24 hours due to the German offensive of the previous day. Once again the attack was preceded by a heavy bombardment by artillery and mortars, but the Germans were well prepared too. As the Scots Guards crossed the shell-pocked open ground north of the railway line they were subjected to a barrage of shells from German artillery. It soon became clear that further progress was impossible, and this – the brigade's fifth assault on the stronghold was eventually called off.

By then the situation facing the Allies had improved. The transports carrying the British 7th Armoured Division had arrived off the beachhead, and soon fresh troops would be able to take over from the battle-scarred survivors of the 56th Division. The British had weathered the storm – but only just. What had saved Graham and his men was the fact that while they had been sorely pressed, the bulk of Gen. Herr's LXXVI Panzer Korps had been occupied attacking the equally hard-pressed troops of the US VI Corps. If the major German counter-attack of 'Black Monday' – 13 February or D+5 – had been thrown into the fight around Battipaglia then the outcome of the Salerno battle might have been very different.

THE STRUGGLE FOR ALTAVILLA

Compared to the struggle facing the British X Corps the expansion of the American bridgehead had gone remarkably well. By dawn on 11 September (D+3) the US VI Corps had bridged the river Sele and the river Calore near Albanella Station, and was well placed for a general advance up the Sele, towards the Ponte Sele, where Highway 9 and the main railway crossed the river. Seizing it would prevent the rest of LXXVI Panzer Korps from reinforcing Sieckenius' 16. Panzer-Division at Battipaglia, but the position could only be held if VI Corps also held the banks of the river Calore and the high ground that overlooked it near Altavilla. The scene was set for one of the most closely fought engagements of the battle.

The previous evening the 142nd RCT captured Albanella, on the far side of Mote Soprano from the beachhead at Paestum. To the north-east lay the high ground around Altavilla which would form the regiment's next objective. In fact the regiment's 2nd Battalion (2/142) had already been moving towards it, but spent the night about 3 miles short of the village, bivouacked on the eastern bank of the La Cosa stream. The following morning they broke camp, and struggled up the hill to Altavilla. The battalion entered the village at noon, and found signs that the Germans had recently occupied it. In fact, the company-strength German garrison from Panzergrenadier-Regiment 15 had been withdrawn earlier that morning. The village lay on the western slopes of Hill 424, so the American battalion commander Lt. Col. Barron established his main defensive position on the summit, a mile to the east of the village. His support company was posted in the village itself.

Meanwhile, down in the Sele Valley on the morning of 11 September the bulk of the 179th RCT of the 45th Division advanced towards Highway 9. The regiment's 2nd Battalion headed towards the bridge spanning the small river Calore, which served the road linking Altavilla and Ponte Sele. It reached it at 1000hrs, but a counter-attack by I/Panzergrenadier-Regiment 15 recaptured the destroyed bridge and the Americans were driven back to the southern bank of the river. While the Germans eventually withdrew, and the 2/179th returned to the northern side of the river, its position remained precarious.

Behind them, the rest of the 179th RCT was also in trouble, as halfway between Persano and Ponte Sele the Germans struck, and soon the Americans found themselves surrounded. Colonel Hutchins of the 179th had bypassed Persano, but it was still held by the Germans, while reinforcements now reached it via the bridge across the river Sele to the west of the small medieval village. Oberst Ulich of the 29. Panzergrenadier-Division attacked the Americans from both front and rear, and his men repulsed all attempts by Hutchins to break through the German blocking force at Persano. The rest of the 45th Division was unable to help as they had problems of their own on the far bank of the river Sele.

Colonel Ankcorn's 157th RCT should have been covering the bridge over the Sele at Persano, but it had been stopped just short of

GIs of the US 36th Infantry Division clamber down landing nets from their transport ship into a Higgins Infantry Landing Craft off Paestum, during the landings at Salerno. The transport appears to be a Landing Ship Tank (LST).

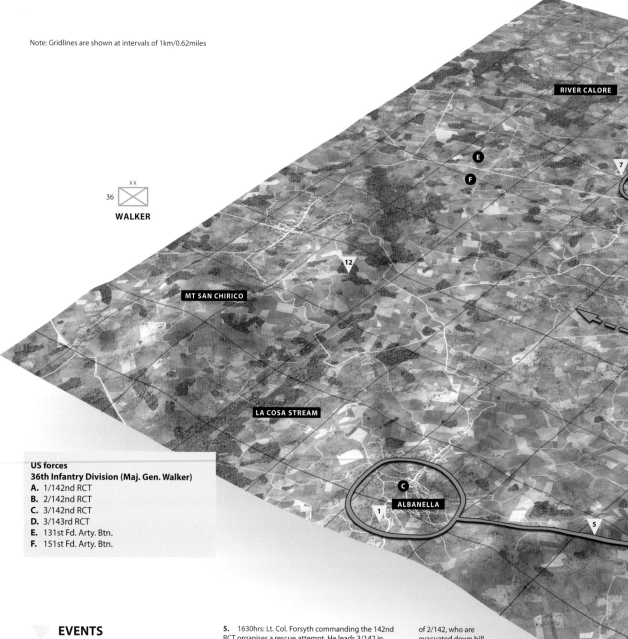

Note: Gridlines are shown at intervals of 1km/0.62miles

RIVER CALORE

E

F

7

36 ⌷ WALKER

12

MT SAN CHIRICO

LA COSA STREAM

US forces
36th Infantry Division (Maj. Gen. Walker)
A. 1/142nd RCT
B. 2/142nd RCT
C. 3/142nd RCT
D. 3/143rd RCT
E. 131st Fd. Arty. Btn.
F. 151st Fd. Arty. Btn.

C

ALBANELLA

1

5

EVENTS

1. 2000hrs, 10 September: 3/142nd RCT occupies Albanalla. Meanwhile 2/142 spends the night bivouacked to east of La Cosa stream. 1/142 held in reserve.

2. 1200hrs, 11 September: having resumed its advance on Altavilla at dawn, 2/142 occupies the village. The German garrison had been withdrawn an hour before. 2/142 digs in on Hill 424, and in village

Sunday 12 September (D+3)

3. 0400: during the night Panzergrenadiers of II/Panzergrenadier-Regiment 15 infiltrate the American positions. They open up with a heavy all-round fire. By 1100hrs German artillery joins in and radio contact with 2/142 is lost.

4. 1300hrs: when battalion commander is killed the battered 2/142 withdraw towards Altavilla, but are cut off and pinned down. The village itself is then attacked and the American garrison driven down the hill.

5. 1630hrs: Lt. Col. Forsyth commanding the 142nd RCT organises a rescue attempt. He leads 3/142 in circuitous route from Albanella to Hill 424, by way of mountainous ridge to the south of Altavilla. Battalion is short of its objective by nightfall, and bivouacs on Hill 423.

6. 1800hrs: 2/179 stationed to north of river Calore is relieved by 3/143, which then receives orders to launch dawn attack on Altavilla and Hill 424, in support of the 3/142's assault.

Monday 13 September (D+4)

7. 0500hrs: 1/142 ordered forward and held in reserve to support rest of 142nd RCT.

8. 0600hrs: 3/142 resumes advance on Hill 424, supported by artillery. They encounter heavy German fire, and local German counter-attacks pin them short of objective. By noon major German counter-attack forces survivors of battalion to withdraw.

9. 0900hrs: having begun advance three hours earlier, 3/143 reaches crest of Hill 424, but German defenders prevent capture of summit. At 1400hrs Altavilla occupied and contact made with survivors

of 2/142, who are evacuated down hill towards 1/142's positions.

10. 1700hrs: Germans attack 3/143's positions and drive battalion down hill towards La Cosa stream. K Company cut off and surrounded in corner of village. Company surrenders the following morning.

11. 1730hrs: having received orders at 1400hrs to work their way around Altavilla to the south, 1/142 is spotted by German observers in newly recaptured Altavilla, and brought under heavy artillery fire. Heavy casualties, and survivors retire to the west.

12. By midnight the remains of the 142nd RCT and 3/143 are behind La Cosa stream, with exception of K/3/143, which is trapped in Altavilla. Under heavy pressure elsewhere, divisional commander of the US 36th Infantry Division abandons attempt to recapture Altavilla.

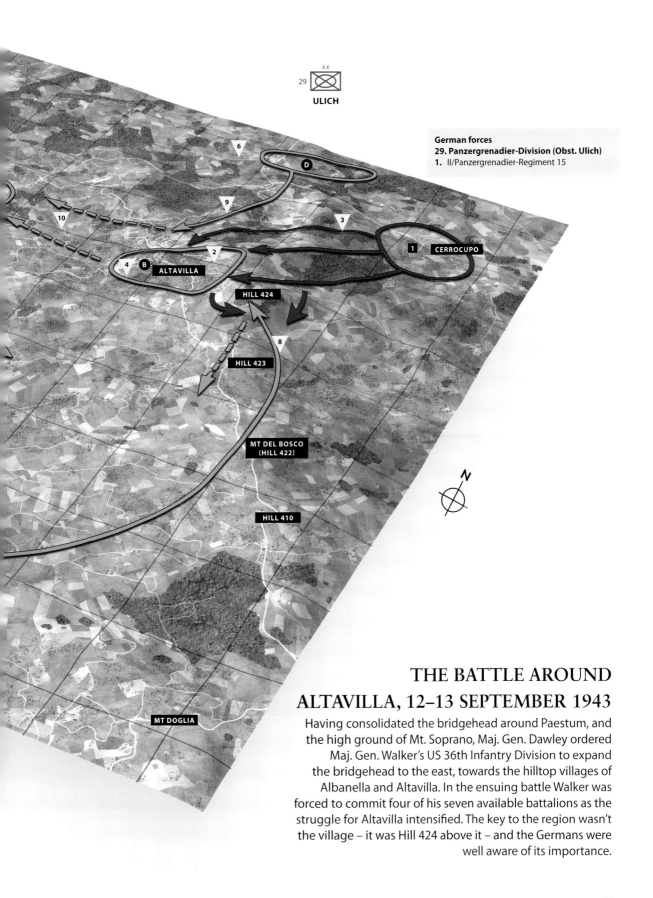

29 · XX · ULICH

German forces
29. Panzergrenadier-Division (Obst. Ulich)
1. II/Panzergrenadier-Regiment 15

6

D

9

10

3

1 CERROCUPO

2

4 B

ALTAVILLA

HILL 424

8

HILL 423

MT DEL BOSCO
(HILL 422)

HILL 410

MT DOGLIA

N

THE BATTLE AROUND ALTAVILLA, 12–13 SEPTEMBER 1943

Having consolidated the bridgehead around Paestum, and the high ground of Mt. Soprano, Maj. Gen. Dawley ordered Maj. Gen. Walker's US 36th Infantry Division to expand the bridgehead to the east, towards the hilltop villages of Albanella and Altavilla. In the ensuing battle Walker was forced to commit four of his seven available battalions as the struggle for Altavilla intensified. The key to the region wasn't the village – it was Hill 424 above it – and the Germans were well aware of its importance.

it at the Fiocche Tobbaco Factory, which dominated the northern and western approaches to the bridge. Kampfgruppe Krüger had occupied the Tobacco Factory earlier that morning, and throughout the day it prevented any attempt by the Americans to advance any further up the northern bank of the Sele.

What finally saved Col. Hutchins' command was the fact that during the night Kampfgruppe Ulich had withdrawn from Persano as the blocking force there was short of ammunition. At 0700hrs the following morning – 12 September – a cautious advance by the tankers of the 753rd Tank Battalion made contact with the beleaguered 179th RCT, and in the process they discovered that Persano had been abandoned. While Hutchins' men recovered from their ordeal, the action switched to the far side of the river Calore, where the 2/142nd was dug in around Altavilla.

During the early hours of Sunday 12th, II/Panzergrenadier-Regiment 15 – part of Kampfgruppe Ulich – approached Hill 424 from the east, and successfully infiltrated the American positions there. At around 0400hrs the Germans opened fire, seemingly from every direction at once. Every defending company found itself isolated. This fire continued all morning, and at 1100hrs German artillery began pounding the hill where the beleaguered Texans of the 2/142nd were pinned down in their foxholes. The battalion commander was killed as he tried to redeploy his men, while his three rifle companies remained pinned down on the hilltop. During the afternoon the Germans infiltrated the village and, as darkness fell, the support company withdrew back down the hill to the west and headed for the safety of the La Casa stream. The Germans pulled back slightly during the night, but the bulk of the 2/142nd still remained trapped.

That afternoon Maj. Gen. Walker realized the seriousness of the situation, and ordered Lt. Col. Forsyth of the 142nd RCT to intervene. At 1630hrs Forsyth led his regiment's 3rd Battalion eastwards from Albanella towards Monte Doglia. His plan was to approach Hill 424 from the south, working his way along the ridgeline to rescue what remained of his beleaguered 2nd Battalion. Meanwhile at the Calore Bridge the battered 2/179th were relieved by the 3rd Battalion of the 143rd RCT, who were given orders to launch a dawn attack on Hill 424 from the north, timed to coincide with Forsyth's attack from the south. Forsyth's men caught a few hours of rest when they reached the ridge, so they would be reasonably fresh for the following morning.

Meanwhile, Walker ordered up two battalions of field artillery, who deployed along the eastern banks of La Calore stream so they could fire in support of the attack. During the night the understrength 1st Battalion of the 142nd RCT was ordered up to screen them and to stand by as the regimental reserve in case it needed to intervene in the coming battle. When dawn broke on 13 September the two Texan battalions – the 3/143rd in the north and the 3/142nd in the south – began their advance. There had been no radio contact with the beleaguered remnants of the 2/142nd since the previous day, so Forsyth would have to use his initiative when he reached his objective. His priorities were to extricate the survivors and to re-establish control of the hilltop.

An artillery bombardment preceded the American attack, and at 0600hrs Forsyth began his advance northwards from Hill 423. By 0700hrs he was halfway to his objective, and his men had just reached an unnamed hill. They suddenly came under machine-gun fire, so Forsyth sent two companies around the right flank of the German position. The three machine-gun nests were silenced, and by 0730hrs the Americans were in possession of the hill.

They were now less than 800 yards south of their objective – the beleaguered men of the 2/142nd.

At that point they were hit by a fierce German artillery barrage, under cover of which the Panzergrenadiers of II/Panzergrenadier-Regiment 15 worked their way between the two halves of Forsyth's force. Eventually the now-isolated L and M Companies of the 3/142nd were forced to pull back and rejoin the rest of the battalion on the northern slopes of Hill 423. The battalion remained pinned down all morning, until a spirited German counter-attack at noon forced them to pull back out of range down the western slopes of the ridge.

After securing the landing beaches at Paestum, American troops expanded their bridgehead. Here, troops from the 45th Division's 179th RCT can be seen marching north out of Paestum along Highway 18. Paestum's Tempio di Cerere can be seen in the background.

Meanwhile, Lt. Col. Barnett's 3/143rd had started climbing the northern slopes of Hill 424 at 0600hrs, and three hours later it reached the crest of the hill. The position was strongly held by German infantry, who defied all attempts by Barnett to eject them. Then, Barnett switched tactics. While artillery pinned down the German defenders he sent one of his companies around the hillside to reach Altavilla. Shortly after 1400hrs the village was occupied and contact was re-established with the 2/142nd, which was pinned down on the south-western slopes of Hill 424. They were evacuated down the hill to the west, towards the safety of the La Cosa stream.

Despite having rescued the beleaguered defenders, Barnett's men were still in a precarious position. They formed part of a pincer movement which had failed, and with the withdrawal of Forsyth's men they were left to their own devices. Colonel Martin of the 143rd RCT realized this and persuaded Maj. Gen. Walker to order forward the 1/142nd, which until now had been held in reserve near the La Cosa stream. It was duly ordered forwards, supported by a company of tanks, with orders to climb the ridge to the south of the village and to re-establish contact between Barnett and Forsyth.

This plan fell apart while these reinforcements were still making their approach march. Shortly before 1700hrs the Panzergrenadiers of II/Panzergrenadier-Regiment 15 attacked down the hill, having spent the previous hour working their way around the flanks of the 3/143rd's positions. Within 30 minutes the battalion broke and ran, fleeing down the hillside to the west, as their route back to the Calore Bridge had now been cut. K Company was still garrisoning Altavilla, but rather than join the rout it held its ground, being driven back into a corner of the village, and surrounded.

Having regained control of most of the village the Germans then spotted the 1/142nd, which was working its way up out of the valley below them. Soon artillery fire from the 29. Panzergrenadier-Division began falling amongst the American troops. They had nowhere to run – artillery observers in Altavilla could see every move they made. As a result the battalion suffered heavy casualties, and soon it too was fleeing back the way it had come.

By nightfall on 13 September the Germans were firmly in control of Altavilla, while the remnants of the shattered 142nd RCT were licking their wounds on the far bank of the La Cosa stream. So too was the 3/143rd,

The village of Altavilla, pictured from the lower portion of the village, looking eastwards towards its highest point. It was in these buildings that the men of K Company of 3/143rd RCT were surrounded by the enemy on the evening of 13 September.

whose K Company was still trapped in Altavilla. It would eventually surrender the following morning. This meant that at a crucial juncture in the battle for the bridgehead, one German battalion had taken on four American battalions and had emerged victorious. Major-General Walker only had eight rifle battalions at his disposal, as the first battalion of the 143rd RCT had been sent north to reinforce the Rangers at the Chiunzi Pass. At a time when every GI was desperately needed, the sacrifice of these four battalions almost cost the Allies the battle.

THE TOBACCO FACTORY

The seeds of 'Black Monday' were sown two days before, when Maj. Gen. Middleton's 45th Division failed to secure the valley of the river Sele. The rough handling of the 179th RCT north of Persano, and the failure of the 157th RCT to secure control of the Tobacco Factory and the nearby bridge over the Sele all contributed to the near-disaster. Kampfgruppe Ulich had withdrawn from Persano during the evening of 11/12 September, and during Sunday it was heavily reinforced. LXXVI Panzer Korps was gathering its forces around Ponte Sele, but, despite the intelligence reports, Maj. Gen. Dawley seemed to be more concerned with reorganizing his corps and divisional boundaries than preparing his front line for a German onslaught. However, the Sunday was a fruitful one as, if nothing else, the Americans had made progress, despite the failure of the 36th Division to hold Altavilla.

First, after the relief column reached the 179th RCT Persano was cleared by engineers and supplies were brought forward. On the north bank of the river Sele the 157th RCT was ordered to take the Tobacco Factory, and the attack began at 0900hrs on Sunday morning, just as the Americans across the river were entering Persano. This time Col. Ankcorn used his whole regiment, supported by the 191st Tank Battalion. The tanks shelled the buildings for over an hour, while the infantry worked their way forwards between the factory and the river and fired at the complex from two sides. When the assault went in it was discovered that the Germans had withdrawn, and so by 1130hrs the Tobacco Factory was safely in American hands.

At 1300hrs the Germans launched a counter-attack. Kampfgruppe von Doering advanced south along the road leading from Eboli and, while eight German tanks occupied the American armour, I/Panzergrenadier-Regiment 79 swept through the Tobacco Factory like a whirlwind and ejected its garrison, the 1/157th. This German success raised the spectre of another German move across the bridge leading to Persano, which would lead to the encirclement of the 179th RCT. The Tobacco Factory had to be retaken, whatever the cost.

Therefore, at 1630hrs the 157th RCT advanced towards the Tobacco Factory for the second time that day, with its 1st and 3rd Battalions taking the lead, each supported by a company of tanks. A chemical mortar battalion laid a smokescreen, and at 1700hrs the GIs reached the buildings. They were deserted – once again the Germans had withdrawn. The 1/157th reoccupied the factory while the 3/157th dug in a little to the north to protect its flank. With this key feature secured, Middleton's 45th Division had secured an important link between its two regiments – one on each bank of the river Sele. The division's third infantry formation, the 180th RCT, was still embarked on the transport ships acting as a floating reserve.

Major-General Dawley must have wondered why the Germans had been so willing to relinquish control of Persano and the Tobacco Factory. He had spent part of this crucial day conferring with Clark discussing boundaries. Originally the boundary of the two Allied corps was to be the river Sele, but with the British still stuck on the river Tusciano there was a 7½-mile gap between the two Allied bridgeheads. The decision was made to extend the corps boundary northwards. To secure this new boundary Dawley sent the 36th Division's engineers northwards to Bivio Cioffi, which was 2½ miles from the nearest British unit at Santa Lucia. This little hamlet would serve as the northern outpost of his bridgehead. That evening he prepared orders to rearrange his dispositions. The 45th Division would be concentrated north of the river Sele, from Bivio Cioffi to the Tobacco Factory. That night, the 179th RCT was ordered to cross the river, a redeployment which was achieved shortly before dawn. The 3/157th was now deployed astride Highway 18, between the 36th Division's engineers at Bivio Cioffi and the 3/157th, dug in north of the Tobacco Factory. The rest of the 179th RCT was placed in reserve 2 miles behind the line, just north of the point where Highway 18 crossed the river Sele.

This left a 2-mile gap in the American line between the Sele and Calore rivers. The only troops in the area were the 3/143rd, guarding the bridge over the Calore to the north of Altavilla. It was already under orders to launch an attack on Altavilla the following morning, so the entire American centre was about to be denuded of troops. To make matters worse, that evening Dawley ordered Walker's 141st RCT, which was in reserve around Albanella Station, to cross the river Sele the following morning and establish a link with the British on the Tusciano. It had been holding the southern flank of the beachhead, but as no attack seemed forthcoming there it was moved north. That left the 3/143rd, which was Walker's last unengaged battalion. Like the 141st RCT it too was being held in reserve on Monte San Chirico, overlooking the La Calore stream. This meant that when the Germans finally launched their counter-attack their task was made much easier thanks to Daley's dispositions.

The Torre di Paestum overlooks the American landing beaches at Peastum, and on the morning of 9 September it was used by German snipers and machine-gunners, who enjoyed a clear field of fire; the sea is just 60 yards from its base. (Charles S. Grant)

'BLACK MONDAY'

During the morning of Monday 13 September the fighting raged on the hills above Albanella, but elsewhere in the VI Corps beachhead the battlefield was surprisingly quiet. This certainly wasn't true further inland around Eboli and Ponte Sele, where four powerful German *Kampfgruppen* were moving into position, while beyond Highway 19 artillerymen were stockpiling shells beside their gun pits. To the east of Battipaglia, Kampfgruppe von Doering of the 16. Panzer-Division was preparing to recapture the Tobacco Factory and pin the US 45th Division north of the river Sele. To guard Doering's right flank, Kampfgruppe Stempel was ordered to launch pinning attacks against the British enclave around Santa Lucia.

The main attack would be launched across the bridge over the Sele, which was merely the first of LXXVI Panzer Korps' objectives that day. General Herr saw the battle for the bridgehead wouldn't be decided in the hills around Altavilla – it was all about controlling bridges. His objective was the two bridges over the Sele at the Tobacco Factory and Albanella Station, and the pontoon bridge over the river Calore south of Persano. With these crossings in German hands the 45th Division would be cut off from its beachhead, and, deprived of its supplies, it could be destroyed at leisure.

To achieve this, the newly formed Kampfgruppe Kleine Limburg was to capture Persano, after securing the bridge beside the Tobacco Factory. The Panzergrenadiers of Kampfgruppe Krüger – part of the 29. Panzergrenadier-Division – would advance down the Sele–Calore corridor to link up with Kleine Limburg's force at Persano. They were allocated two Panzer companies as support. Finally Kampfgruppe Ulich of the same division would occupy the Americans in the hills above Altavilla, and act as a reserve if required.

Early that morning, Dawley must have realized that Persano was unguarded. Therefore he ordered the 2/143rd – Walker's last reserve – to cross the river Calore and take up a defensive position north of Persano. This would place the battalion directly in the path of Kampfgruppe Krüger. Lieutenant-Colonel Jones, who commanded the battalion, was in position by 0730hrs. His men dug in, with G Company deployed in forward outposts in front of his main line. Across the river Sele, Col. Ankcorn of the 157th RCT was ordered to use his 1st Battalion to clear the Grataglia Woods, a mile up the Eboli road from the Tobacco Factory. This was an impressive name for the small patch of woodland that bordered the narrow road. The operation got underway at 1100hrs, and by noon the advance had halted as German resistance proved tougher than had been anticipated. The reason soon became clear. Spotter planes reported a concentration of German tanks and armour a mile to the north, between the road and the Torre Palladino.

The German assault began with a shelling of the 1/157th clustered around the Grataglia woods. Then a German combined arms attack pinned the battalion in place while more German infantry from Kampfgruppe von Doering worked their way around its right flank, moving between the woods and the river. The Americans were driven off to the east, but reformed near the Fiocche Farm where, covered by the 3/157th, they dug in north of the Tobacco Factory. Others withdrew to the factory itself. This left the road clear, and Hauptmann Kleine Limburg raced south to seize the Sele Bridge supported by a company of tanks from Kampfpgruppe von Doering.

Behind them came the rest of Doering's Panzers, supported by I/Panzergrenadier-Regiment 79. Their objective was the Tobacco Factory, which was captured after a brief struggle. However, any attempt to venture any further down the road was met by fire from the 753rd Tank Battalion, deployed to the south-west of the factory. Meanwhile II/Panzergrenadier-Regiment 79 drove the remnants of the 1/157th from Fiocche Farm, The 3/157th had expected any German attack to come from the north, down Highway 18. Their entrenchments were therefore poorly placed to stop an attack from the east. Fortunately for them, the anticipated assault never came. After securing his main objectives, Doering pulled back his tanks so they could add their weight to what Gen. Herr had envisioned as the key area of the battlefield – the area between the river Calore and the sea.

After securing the Sele Bridge, Kleine Limburg pushed past Persano to fall upon the rear of Lt. Col. Jones' battalion. No sooner had the Americans turned to face this unexpected threat than Kampfgruppe Krüger launched its attack, hitting them from the front. G Company fled south towards the bridge over the Calore leading to Altavilla – the one the 3/142nd had attacked Altavilla from that morning. The rest of the battalion was surrounded and destroyed, losing 508 men killed or captured in less than 30 minutes. With Jones' force dealt with, once Krüger and Kleine Limburg secured their prisoners they were then free to continue on down the Sele–Calore corridor, towards Albanella Station and the American beaches.

It was now later afternoon – around 1700hrs. Doering crossed the Sele Bridge and was reunited with the Panzer company he had lent to Kleine Limburg. He now had a force of around 15 tanks at his disposal – most of which were PzKpfw IVs. His Panzergrenadiers were still on the north bank of the river Sele, and Krüger's men were still on the far side of Persano. Doering decided to press on with his tanks alone, hoping to seize the two American pontoon bridges over the Calore by *coup de main* before the Americans had time to react. In fact the Americans were ready and waiting.

On the far bank, two American field artillery battalions were deployed – the 158th and the 189th – and these guns laid down a furious barrage in the path of the advancing German armour. The crews had already been stripped of men, as many of the gunners were deployed behind the river armed with rifles and machine guns. While staff officers combed the beachhead for anyone who could carry a rifle, these men were charged with holding the line. Their task was made much simpler a few minutes later, when engineers blew up the two pontoon bridges. This meant that the Panzers were unable to cross the river unless they could find a ford. Seven M7 self-propelled guns, a handful of M10 tank destroyers, and six obsolete 37mm anti-tank guns soon joined the defenders.

German prisoners pressed into service by the Americans to unload supplies and transport the wounded on the Paestum beachhead during the early days of the fighting. On D+2 a POW holding area was established beside the ruins of Paestum.

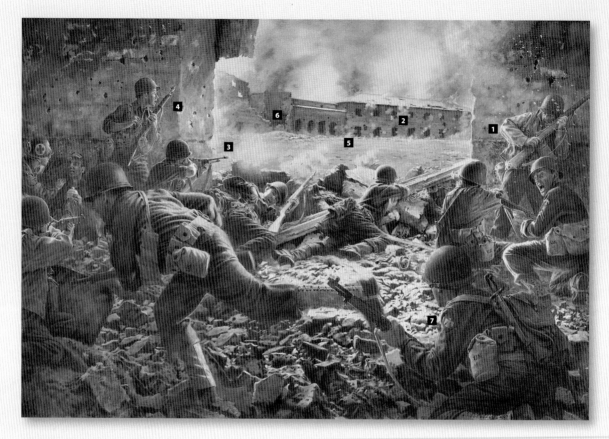

THE FIGHT FOR THE TOBACCO FACTORY, VI CORPS SECTOR, D+3, 1330HRS (pp. 74–75)

On 11 September, when the US 45th Infantry Division tried to expand the American bridgehead to the north, it found its path blocked by the Tabacchificio Fiocche. This large circular tobacco factory acted like a ready-made fortress, and dominated the north bank of the river Sele to the east of Highway 18. It also guarded the bridge across the river near Persano. If the landing beaches were to be protected then the Tobacco Factory had to be captured. The 157th RCT failed to take it that evening, so a better-planned assault was scheduled for the following morning. At 1000hrs on 12 September the regiment attacked again, supported by tanks and artillery. When the assault was launched it was discovered that the German defenders had withdrawn, and so by 1130hrs the complex was in American hands. It was garrisoned by the 1st Battalion of the 157th. Then, at 1300hrs the Germans counter-attacked, supported by tanks. After a short, sharp fight the Americans were ejected from the building, which had to be retaken by the 1/157th later that afternoon. The Tobacco Factory

would change hands twice more before the end of the battle.

Here, GIs of the 1/157th (1) hold a shell-damaged warehouse on the western edge of the large circular complex. Panzergrenadiers from I/Panzergrenadier-Regiment 79 of the 16. Panzer-Division have already recaptured the buildings on the eastern side of the factory (2), and are using automatic weapons to suppress the American defenders. A BAR gunner (3) and the squad's riflemen armed with M1 Garand rifles (4) are attempting to return fire as best they can. While this exchange is taking place, German Panzergrenadiers are working their way around the circular complex, avoiding the circular central loading area (5), but instead working their way anti-clockwise around it, using the tobacco warehouses as cover (6). The hard-pressed GIs are lightly equipped and wear the 'Thunderbird' patch of the 45th Infantry Division (7) on their shoulder. When the German attackers reach their warehouse these GIs will be forced to withdraw to the west, leaving the battered factory to the Germans.

During the attack the gunners were firing eight rounds a minute, and together the 24 guns of the 158th and 189th fired 3,650 rounds that evening. Eventually, after milling around for 30 minutes without finding a place to cross, the German tanks withdrew leaving at least two damaged tanks behind them. Doering hoped he would be able to renew the assault the following morning once he had infantry and engineers to support him. In fact, the unsupported assault by his Panzers represented the high water mark of the German counter-attack.

That evening there was little sense of exultation in Dawley's headquarters. At the height of the attack, when Lt. Gen. Clark asked him what he planned to do, Dawley replied 'Nothing. I've no reserves. All I've got is a prayer.' Clark was singularly unimpressed. During the day Walker had lost two battalions around Altavilla and one north of Persano. Middleton's 1/157th was badly battered, and if the Germans renewed the attack the following morning there was every chance that they would be able to reach Paestum. It is little wonder that American historians dubbed 13 September 'Black Monday'.

THE TIDE TURNS

As dawn broke on 14 September there was no sense in the Allied camp that the corner had been turned. Lieutenant-General Clark had spent the night considering the possibility of withdrawal, but decided against it. At least he knew that reinforcements were on their way. The previous afternoon Maj. Gen. Ridgeway, commanding the US 82nd Airborne Division based in Sicily had agreed to drop one of his parachute infantry regiments within the American beachhead that evening, and to land the rest of his division on following evenings. So, at 2100hrs, all anti-aircraft guns fell silent and landing markers were lit on the ground. The first drop went well – two battalions of Col. Tucker's 504th PIR landed safely between Paestum and Albanella Station. The second lift was mishandled, and the 3/504th was hopelessly scattered all over the Salerno Plain, with most of the men falling behind enemy lines.

While the infantry fought their way of the landing beaches at Paestum, medical teams did what they could to cope with the steady flow of casualties. Here a medical team from the 4th Naval Battalion has just examined the body of a young Texan GI, killed beside a radio jeep.

Still, Dawley and Walker now had two fresh and veteran battalions, and these were rushed into the front line, ready to face a dawn attack.

At Paestum, Maj. Gen. Walker reorganized what remained of his division, and replaced all three of his regimental commanders. The remnants of the 143rd RCT were given to Brig. Gen. Wilbur, while Col. Lange was given two companies of the 141st, and the 1st and 2nd Battalions of the 504th PIR. Brigadier-General Daniel assumed command of the rest of the division's infantry. Strangely, the original regimental commanders remained on as their replacements' second in command.

Americans being transferred from a transport ship to a tank landing ship off the Paestum beachhead on 10 September. During the battle for the beachhead trucks like these proved extremely useful ferrying troops and supplies around the cramped American bridgehead.

The 142nd RCT was withdrawn to the beachhead to recover, so the line along the La Cosa stream was held by the 2/141st, two battalions of the 504th PIR and the 1/141st on the far right of the line, supported by shore engineers brought up from the beaches. The line was stiffened by elements of the 751st Tank Battalion and the 636th Tank Destroyer Battalion.

The Germans resumed their offensive on the morning of 14 September, but surprisingly the action started around Bivio Cioffi, rather than at the Calore Bridge. At 0800hrs Kampfgruppe van Doering attacked using the I/Panzergrenadier-Regiment 79 supported by two Panzer companies. They approached from Fiocche Farm, to the north of the German-held Tobacco Factory, then veered southwards towards the bridge leading to Albanella Station. Two battalions of the 179th RCT, supported by tanks and anti-tank guns, held the line there. Within 30 minutes seven of the German tanks were destroyed, and, while the Panzergrenadiers continued to attack, the assault was called off at 0930hrs. During the early afternoon two further battalion-sized attacks on Bivio Cioffi were repulsed, as was a probe down the north banks of the river Sele from the Tobacco Factory to the Highway 18 bridge over the river. In all these attacks, a combination of artillery fire and naval gunnery played a major part in deterring the Germans.

Further to the south German dawn patrols had probed the American line along the river Calore and the La Cosa stream, and by 0900hrs this had developed into a full-scale assault. A Panzergrenadier battalion from Kampfgruppe Krüger tried to ford the Calore around the destroyed bridge, supported by a company of tanks, but the assault was easily repulsed by the infantry, supported by tanks and tank destroyers firing from hull down positions. The attack was renewed at 1300hrs, but this second combined arms assault was also driven back with heavy losses. One M10 of the 636th Tank Destroyer Battalion called 'Jinx' destroyed five German tanks during the attack. German probes and minor attacks continued until nightfall, but it was fast becoming clear that the American defences were now too strong for the Germans to break.

The German counter-attack, 12–14 September 1943

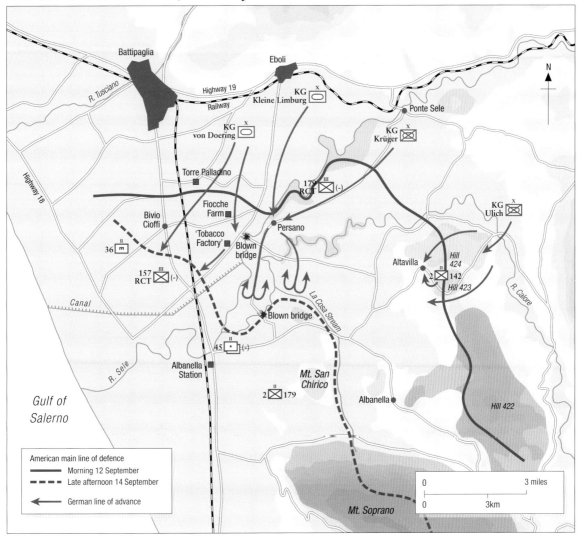

While fighting still raged along the Tusciano, the main crisis in the British sector early on 14 September came when the Germans assaulted 'White House Hill'. The previous day Brig. James' 128th Brigade had rotated with the battered 139th brigade, occupying its positions on the hill. The Commando Brigade was also available as a reserve, based at Mercatello. The German attack began with a heavy *Nebelwerfer* barrage just as the forward companies were being rotated with those held behind the crest in reserve. Casualties were therefore unusually heavy. By 0100hrs German infantry began infiltrating the British positions, which were already in some disorder due to the bombardment.

The result was that Kampfgruppe Stroh overran the positions of the 1/4th Hampshires, and within an hour the eastern and central portions of the ridge were in German hands. On its western end facing Salerno the 5th Hampshires found themselves pinned down and unable to move. The following morning – 15 September – the Germans assaulted the stranded battalion, and by

1100hrs its survivors were withdrawing back towards Mercatello. The loss of 'White House Hill' was a major blow for McCreery. It meant that German artillery observers now had a clear view of the British beaches and could call down artillery fire wherever they liked. The fighting in the British sector over the next few days would be dominated by the struggle to retake the ridge.

For McCreery, this blow was tempered by the realization that the chaotic fighting along the river Tusciano had stabilized slightly, and by 15 September the arrival of the 7th Armoured Division meant that the exposed flank beyond the Fosso Bridge could be made reasonably secure. Kampfgruppe Sempel had been badly battered during the week's fighting, and when it pulled back to regroup the British reoccupied San Mattia and strengthened the defences linking the Fosse Bridge to Santa Lucia. That evening Kampfgruppe Krüger moved from Persano to Battipaglia to replace Sempel's troops in the front line.

On 16 September it launched a two-battalion dawn assault on the British positions around San Mattia, having sent small groups forward to infiltrate the British line before the attack was launched. Eventually the Germans were driven back by a combination of a defensive barrage and a counter-attack by the Coldstream Guards, supported by the Scots Greys. The British tankers then continued on as far as the outskirts of Battipaglia, where they ran into a screen of anti-tank guns and were forced to withdraw. This attack marked the last German assault on the Tusciano. Its failure demonstrated that the easy German victories of the previous week were now in the past. Both the British and the Americans now had enough reserves to prevent any German breakthrough.

One of the main reasons for this Allied success – and for many of the German setbacks of the battle – was the ability of the Allies to direct a heavy defensive barrage of artillery wherever it was needed. The Allied divisions had their own healthy supply of integral artillery, and these could be used to devastating effect. This was particularly true in the British sector, where the

The Fiocche Tobacco Factory, which changed hands several times during the battle around the American beachhead. This photograph taken after the battle shows the complex from the south – the Sele Bridge is approached via the 'T' junction at the bottom right.

gunners were well versed in laying down divisional and even corps-sized defensive barrages. Even more decisive was the firepower provided by the ships of Vice Admiral Hewitt's Western Naval Task Force. In particular, the 6in. guns of the four light cruisers lying off each of the two Allied bridgeheads proved invaluable, as did the 15in. guns of the two British monitors. Their fire was directed by naval gunfire teams sent ashore from the fleet, by spotting aircraft circling the battlefield or, *in extremis*, by the brigade-level staff on the ground, who speedily forwarded requests and coordinates for naval gunfire when they needed it.

The ruins of the 'Tobacco Factory' between Bellizzi and Battipaglia, photographed after the battle. In fact this walled complex of buildings wasn't a tobacco factory at all – it was a collection of agricultural and light industrial workshops and warehouses.

This firepower came at a price. During the battle the ships of the task force were forced to operate in the confined waters of the Gulf of Salerno, and, despite the air cover provided by the support carrier force and the covering carrier force, they were extremely vulnerable to air attack. The first casualty was the light cruiser USS *Savannah*, whose forward turrets were hit by a glide bomb on the morning of 11 September. Two days later the packed hospital ship *Newfoundland* was hit, causing heavy casualties, as was the light cruiser HMS *Uganda*. Both of the light cruisers were able to limp away to safety, but the *Newfoundland* was lost. The most serious naval casualty was the battleship HMS *Warspite*, which arrived off the beachhead late on 15 September, accompanied by the battleship HMS *Valiant*. At 1420hrs the following day *Warspite* was hit by a glide bomb that wrecked her boiler room and caused heavy flooding. The venerable old battleship was towed away to Malta.

A US Ranger watches naval artillery fall on suspected German positions in the mountains flanking the Chiunzi Pass. While the Rangers were unable to prevent the enemy traversing the Nocera Defile, they successfully blocked any German attempt to reach the Amalfi coast.

These German successes were due to the deployment of a relatively new kind of weapon. The Fritz X glide bomb which damaged the *Warspite* and the *Savannah* was launched from a Dornier Do-217 at 10,000ft and was guided to its target using a radio control system. It had a range of 3½ miles, a speed of 550mph and carried a 100kg armour-piercing warhead. The advantage of these weapons was that they could be launched well before the bombers reached their targets,

KAMPFGRUPPE VON DOERING'S ATTACK, SELE–CALORE CORRIDOR, D+4, 1830HRS (pp. 82–83)

13 September was dubbed 'Black Monday' by American historians, as it marked the lowest ebb of fortune for the US VI Corps. That was the day the German LXXVI Panzer Korps launched its major counter-attack against the American beachhead. After recapturing the Tobacco Factory and overrunning an American battalion near Persano, all that lay between the Germans and the landing beaches was a hastily assembled line of American artillery and anti-tank guns sited behind the river Calore, close to where it flowed into the river Sele. Having secured the Tobacco Factory, Kampfgruppe von Doering crossed the river Sele then advanced down the Sele–Calore corridor. Rather than wait for infantry support, Oberst von Doering decided to attack using his armour, hoping to seize the two pontoon bridges across the using speed and surprise.

Here, the leading tanks of his improvised *Kampfgruppe* are seen approaching the river Calore, whose banks are marked by a line of trees **(1)**. By this stage the attack had already been rendered a failure, as US Engineers had just blown up the two bridges **(2)** rather than let them fall into German hands. On the high ground behind the river, American 105mm howitzers of the 158th and 159th Field Artillery Battalions **(3)** are firing on the German tanks, and have already caused some damage on them through scoring direct hits. A PzKpfw IV tank has caught fire **(4)**, and its commander is clambering out of the turret to extinguish the flames. The leading German tank **(5)** has just been knocked out by the fire from American anti-tank guns and armour, sited on the far bank of the small river **(6)**. Interestingly, while these PzKpfw IVs have been fitted with protective turret skirts **(7)**, their side skirts have been left off, as it was found that they were a liability in narrow Italian roads. These tanks all bear the marking of the 16. Panzer-Division, and formed part of its Panzer-Regiment 2.

and the controlling aircraft could then hide behind its fighter escort while the bomb was guided onto its target.

This also highlights another problem facing the Allies. Although they had 1,395 fighters and fighter-bombers at their disposal, as well as 1,336 medium and heavy bombers, these had to fly from airfields in Sicily, and so, even with extra fuel tanks, the fighters only had a very limited flying time over the Salerno battlefield. The German airfields around Foggia were only ten minutes away in a German fighter. The turning point in the air war came on 11 September, when an allied airfield opened at Paestum. By 15 September two other airfields were opened in the British sector, which ensured the Allies could guarantee air superiority over the battlefield. This meant that protection could be afforded to Allied bombers, who could then pound the Germans in Battipaglia, Eboli and Ponte Sele, while fighters and fighter-bombers strafed targets of opportunity. The air attack that crippled *Warspite* was the last major German air attack on the beachhead.

That coincided with a general impression that the tide was turning. On the evening of 14 September the 404th PIR landed safely inside the American beachhead, while earlier that day the missing 180th RCT of the 45th Division arrived in its transports, and was transported onto the landing beach at Paestum. This gave the Americans five fresh battalions, plus a battalion of parachute field artillery. An even more ambitious drop of a parachute battalion at Avellino, 25 miles north of Salerno proved to be a disaster, and most of these men, sent as a 'blocking force', were eventually captured by the Germans.

On the strategic level the news from the south was good, as Montgomery's Eighth Army was gradually working its way northwards and had reportedly reached Sapri, 40 miles from the American beaches. Two days later a patrol from the 36th Division encountered the lead units of the British 5th Division at Vallo, which was 18 miles from Paestum. The same day a jeep-load of journalists drove up Highway 18 from Sapri and reached Dawley's headquarters that evening. The road was empty of German troops.

The Germans were still there, facing the two battered Allied corps in the Salerno plain, but there was no sign that they were willing to renew their attacks of the past few days. In fact, patrols from the 36th Division sent forward from the La Cosa position found that the Germans had withdrawn from the Sele–Calore corridor below Persano. I/Panzergrenadier-Regiment 79 was sent forward to form a new line between the two rivers, a mile from Persano. Still, as long as the Germans held the Tobacco Factory and Altavilla the Americans were unable to expand their bridgehead any further. Therefore the decision was made to launch a fresh attack on the hilltop village.

For much of 16 September the 1st and 2nd Battalions of the 82nd Airborne Division's 304th PIR worked their way forwards to Albanella, which was reoccupied late that afternoon. Colonel Tucker had already been briefed on the situation around Altavilla by survivors of the 142nd RCT, and was well aware what to expect there. His plan called for a night assault on Hill 424 from the south, but the battalions soon became lost on the ridge, and were spotted by the Germans, who shelled them. Tucker raced forward to halt his men, and decided to bivouac on Monte del Bosco and resume the assault in the morning.

Heavy shelling continued through the night, but at dawn Tucker resumed the advance and soon patrols of both sides were clashing on the southern slopes of Hill 424 and the unnamed hill beside it where Forsyth's troops of the 36th Division had come to grief four days before. Tucker ordered a bombardment of the hill, but the Panzergrenadiers of II/Panzergrenadier-Regiment 15 struck first, launching a furious assault which sent Tucker's 2nd Battalion reeling backwards until it reached the positions held by the 1st Battalion. The German attacks continued, supported by at least four tanks and assault guns, but a combination of determination and firepower helped the American paratroopers hold their ground.

Eventually the Germans withdrew, and subjected Tucker's men to another night of heavy shelling. When the dawn came on 18 September Tucker fully expected the Germans to attack again. When they didn't materialize he sent out patrols to find out where the enemy were. They found that the Germans had withdrawn during the night, leaving just a small rearguard behind them. By 1500hrs that afternoon the battle-scarred village of Altavilla was back in American hands. That morning American patrols also found the Germans had abandoned the Tobacco Factory and Persano. Both of these key locations were cleared of booby traps, and duly occupied without a shot being fired. It seemed as if all along the VI Corps' front the Germans had withdrawn from the strongpoints they had fought so hard to retain for the past week.

The British were less fortunate on 'White House Hill', a ridge which was becoming as much of an obsession for the British as Altavilla had become for the Americans. On the afternoon of 15 September the Germans ejected the 5th Hampshires from the western end of the ridge and captured the hamlet of Piegollele, which lay to the south of 'The Pimple', the dominant conical hill which marked the eastern end of 'White House Hill'. The Commandos were ordered to retake both Piegollele and 'The Pimple'. As Brig. Laycock was ill, Lt. Col. Churchill led the attack, which began at 1730hrs. While 41 RM Commando secured 'The Crag', a dominant hill to the south of the village, No. 2 Commando captured the village, and then continued on to 'The Pimple'. By 2100hrs it too was in British hands. The plan was to let the 169th Brigade of the 56th Division occupy the ground, and so the Commandos withdrew. However, before the Londoners could reach them the Germans reoccupied the ground. This meant that the Commandos would have to go in again.

The medieval walls of Persano, viewed from the south, and the road which enters the Sele–Calore corridor by way of the Sele Bridge, near the Tobacco Factory. This small town was the scene of heavy fighting on 'Black Monday', 13 September.

41 RM Commando still held 'The Crag' (now dubbed 'Commando Hill'), so Churchill divided No. 2 Commando into two forces. Two troops led by the Duke of Wellington would assault 'The Pimple', while the rest would re-take Piegollele. Due to a radio error Wellington was recalled before he reached his objective and the Commandos returned to their start lines. Another assault was launched at dawn on 16 September, but it was repulsed – the Duke of Wellington being killed during the attack. 'The Pimple' and Piegolelle remained in German hands. During the day Kampfgruppe Stroh attacked 41 RM Commando on 'Commando Hill', but the German attack was repelled. Both sides were now badly battered, but seemed determined to continue the fight.

Wearing a beret, Lt. Gen. McCreery briefs staff of the British Commando Brigade before the attack on Piegolelle and 'The Pimple'. The figure in the foreground is Lt. Col. Churchill, the commander of No. 2 (Army) Commando.

By 17 September the Germans had broken contact with the US VI Corps, but were in action against X Corps. Lieutenant-General McCreery decided to launch another assault on 'White House Hill', and Hawkesworth moved the 138th Brigade over from Dragonea to spearhead the assault, their positions there taken over by the US 325th Glider Regiment. This redeployment took too long to complete, so McCreery ordered the Commandos to lead the attack. This time 41 RM Commando led the assault at 0200hrs, advancing behind a full corps-sized barrage.

Piegollele was found to be abandoned and was reoccupied, and the Commandos continued on up the hill. Then, as they neared their objective the barrage fell short and hit the leading wave of Commandos. One troop reached 'The Pimple' and held it against enemy counter-attacks until 1000hrs the following morning (18 September), when they were forced to withdraw due to lack of ammunition. The fight for 'The Pimple' had cost the British dear. Therefore, it seemed all the more poignant when the following morning they discovered that the Germans had abandoned it during the night, along with the rest of the shell-ravaged 'White House Hill'.

This was the last action of the battle – a fight that had raged for nine days. On the same morning as the Commandos were storming 'The Pimple', the Scots Guards launched another assault against the 'Tobacco Factory', only to find the defenders had gone. Patrols sent forward by the Coldstream Guards continued on into Battipaglia, whose mangled streets were deserted, apart from numerous bodies and a handful of wounded. For the generals, this was something of an embarrassment. The Germans had successfully disengaged without the Allies knowing about it. Any idea of pinning them between the beachhead and Montgomery's advancing troops had evaporated. For the ordinary soldiers though, the end of the fighting could only have come as a blessed relief.

AFTERMATH

General von Vietinghoff gave orders for the German withdrawal at 1700hrs on 17 September. His men had fought well, but to delay any longer risked being caught between Clark and Montgomery's forces. It was an orderly, phased withdrawal, beginning in the south, opposite US VI Corps, followed by the centre around Battipaglia. The German forces in the north would stay where they were and effectively act as the hinge as the German line swung northwards to span the Italian Peninsula to the east of Naples. The whole army would then withdraw northwards to take up position behind the river Volturno, north of Naples. The withdrawal began that evening, although the troops on Hill 424 remained in place the following morning to prevent the Americans from overlooking Pont de Sele while the bulk of LXXVI Panzer Korps passed through it.

The 16. and 26. Panzer-Divisionen and the 29. Panzergrenadier-Division withdrew up the valley of the river Sele past Contursi and Oliveto, before striking northwards to reach Benevento. The 15. Panzergrenadier-Division formed the rearguard. To the east 1. Fallschirmjäger-Division would abandon Foggia, and take up position behind the Sangro River. The withdrawal was conducted with such stealth and efficiency that the Allies were unaware that the Germans had gone until late the following morning – 18 September. The illusion was helped by the tenacity with which the Germans still held 'White House Hill' on the northern flank of the battlefield.

The pursuit: GIs from the US 3rd Infantry Division advancing northwards from Battipaglia in pursuit of the retreating Germans. The division arrived too late to take part in the fight for the Salerno beachhead, but it played a prominent part in the Allied advance to the river Volturno.

Two days after the Germans abandoned the town, Lt. Gen. Clark tours the ruins of Battipaglia, accompanied by Air Chief Marshal Tedder RAF and Maj. Gen. House USAAF. The town was heavily bombed during the closing stages of the battle.

With the Germans having broken contact, Lt. Gen. Clark's first priority should have been to set off in pursuit. Instead, he lingered to witness the landing of the US 3rd Division at Paestum on 19 September, and to pen a letter of commendation to everyone under his command. He specifically highlighted the efficiency of VI Corps, but on 20 September he called Maj. Gen. Dawley to his headquarters and summarily relieved him of his command. Clark was well aware that by his performance at Salerno he had left himself open to criticism. Dawley provided a ready scapegoat. Major-General John Lucas took over from Dawley and would command VI Corps until Clark needed another scapegoat during the Anzio campaign.

The US 45th Division followed the Germans up Highway 19 from Ponte Sele to Oliveto, where they encountered the German rearguard. After two days of fighting the road was cleared and Middleton's men continued on to San Angelo, where the road led to Avellino and Melfi. Its capture secured Montgomery's advance on Foggia, whose airfields were taken on 27 September. Lucas placed the battered US 36th Division in reserve, and instead sent the fresh US 3rd Division up the Tusciano Valley beyond Battipaglia. After a tough fight with a German rearguard near Ancerno, the division eventually reached Highway 7 on 27 September. The two American divisions eventually reached Benevento on 2 October. Their advance had been a frustrating one, as German rearguards, booby traps and demolished bridges had slowed progress to a crawl.

The British X Corps had a tougher time of it as they were advancing against the 'hinge' of the German line, and the Germans fought fiercely. Cava was captured on 19 September, and the British 46th Division slowly worked its way forward until they reached the slopes of Mount Vesuvius. The Germans also slowed the advance of the British 56th Division up the road from Salerno to Avellino. It was a slow, methodical advance carried out by men who had already been through ten days of heavy fighting. It was the end of September before X Corps entered the plain east of Naples and the 7th Armoured Division could take over the advance. After the Germans withdrew from their lines around Mount Vesuvius they pulled back through Naples, and the Allies entered the city on 1 October. On 6 October the Allies had reached the line of the river Volturno, which the Germans held in strength.

The dreadful winter campaign along the Volturno and the bitter battle of Cassino lay ahead. Both sides had been badly drained by the Salerno fighting and needed time to recover their strength and fighting ability. For the moment the soldiers in both armies were content that they had survived the horrors of Salerno. The Allies lost approximately 12,560 men killed, wounded or captured during the battle. German casualties have been placed at around 3,500 to 4,000. In terms of numbers, the Germans did well.

As the German AOK 10 diary put it, 'Though victory was denied, the Tenth Army and its divisions had registered a defensive success under difficult conditions, with almost no air support and under fire of a strong fleet and a powerful air force. The enemy had hoped that German resistance would quickly collapse... Instead he was forced to fight a tough opponent for every yard of territory and use up valuable troops in a minor theatre of war.' That was certainly true – Salerno had been a brutal and hard-fought affair. While the battle had no clear victor, the tactical successes of the Germans were balanced and even outweighed by the strategic results of the battle. The most important of these was that by its end an Allied army was firmly established on Italian soil.

The railway yard at Battipaglia, which was virtually destroyed during Allied bombing raids between 15 and 17 September. The town itself was badly damaged, and the Allies noted that the bombing had also caused heavy German casualties.

The German withdrawal and the Allied pursuit, 15 September–8 October 1943

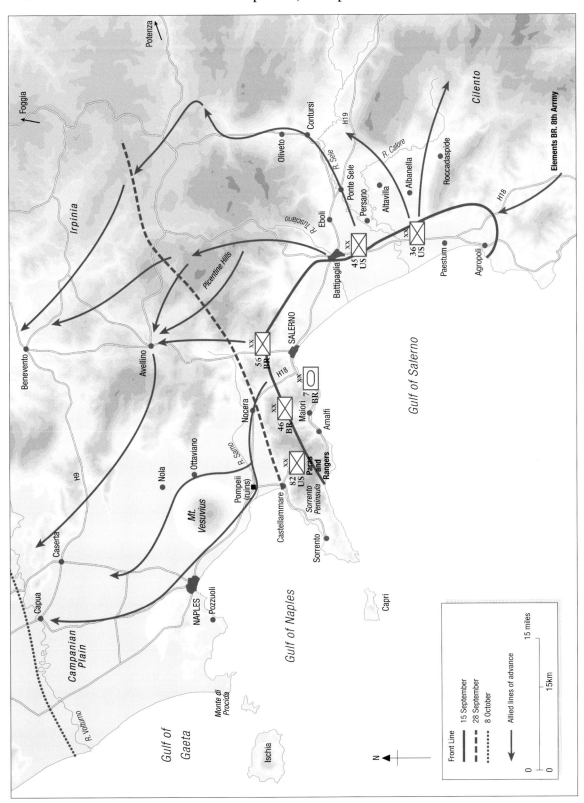

Potenza

Foggia

Irpinia

Contursi

Oliveto

R. Sele

H19

R. Calore

Cilento

Albanella

Roccadaspide

Elements BR. 8th Army

Ponte Sele

Persano

Altavilla

Eboli

R. Tusciano

Battipaglia

45 US

36 US

H18

Paestum

Agropoli

Picentine Hills

Benevento

Avellino

SALERNO

56 BR

Gulf of Salerno

H18

7 BR

Nocera

46 BR

Maiori

Amalfi

R. Sarno

Ottaviano

H9

Nola

Pompeii (ruins)

Mt. Vesuvius

82 US

Paras and Rangers

Sorrento Peninsula

Castellammare

Sorrento

Caserta

NAPLES

Pozzuoli

Capri

Capua

Campanian Plain

Monte di Procida

Gulf of Naples

Gulf of Gaeta

Ischia

R. Volturno

N

Front Line

15 September
28 September
8 October
Allied lines of advance

0   15km
0   15 miles

THE BATTLEFIELD TODAY

One of the real attractions of the Salerno battlefield today is that for the most part it remains unspoiled. Certainly the urban boundaries of Salerno have expanded considerably since September 1943 – new motorways have been cut through the mountain passes to the north and smart villas dot the slopes of 'White House Hill'. The port has expanded and now curves around the bay as far as Vietri. A sea wall and seasonal beach clubs and resorts now line the beaches where X Corps landed, while ugly industrial buildings line the motorway that has replaced the old Highways 18 and 19 running between Salerno and Battipaglia. However, setting this inevitable change aside, many of the places which were so hotly fought over during the battle have remained largely unchanged.

In X Corps sector, Dragonea Hill, 'Monument Hill' and 'Hospital Hill' look much as they did in 1943. On the latter, visitors can even walk the grounds of the hospital whose façade has remained largely unchanged since

The sea front of Salerno as it appears today. Behind the monument lies a modern container port, which stretches along the coast as far as Vietri, which can be seen behind the monument, immediately to its left. On its right is 'Monument Hill'.

the war. They can also saunter through Piegollele, before venturing up the unspoiled slopes of 'The Pimple' and 'Commando Hill'. Further south, the Fosse Bridge is still there – ignored by all but the most local of motorists, as is the village of Santa Lucia. Look hard enough and you can still see the scars of the fighting on some of the older buildings. Montecorvino Airfield is still in use, and light planes still operate from its single runway. You can still drive up 'Grenadier Lane', but locating the 'Tobacco Factory' is more problematic as it no longer retains its wartime appearance, and the site itself in the outskirts of Bellizzi it is now surrounded by a modern industrial sprawl. This area also contains many of the cemeteries where the dead of both sides are buried. These well-tended graves serve to remind us of the human cost of the human cost of the battle, and of the legacy these young men have left behind.

The American beachhead has altered even less than the British one. The ruins of Paestum are still there, and most tourists who visit its temples are unaware that they once housed German machine-gun teams. The Torre di Paestum still overlooks the beach, and the American landing beaches, which were once raked by gunfire, are now the preserve of holidaymakers. To the north and east the countryside remains largely unchanged, save for new housing below Monte San Chirico. The medieval walls of Persano remain untouched, and you can still drive up the winding road to Altavilla. From there visitors can climb through the olive groves to reach Hill 424 and enjoy the view over the landing beaches which made the hilltop such an important objective. However, of all the extant reminders of the battle, the Fiocche Tobacco Factory is the most poignant. The large battle-scarred circular stone structure is now abandoned, and its warehouses are now just roofless shells, but that just adds to its aura – as a battlefield ruin it is just as evocative as Hougoumont or La Haie Sainte.

The remains of the western side of the Fiocche Tobacco Factory today, viewed from the road running along the Sele River, between Eboli and the bridge where Highway 18 crossed the river Sele. The building complex has remained largely unchanged since the war.

FURTHER READING

Ball, Edmund, *Staff Officer with the Fifth Army: Sicily, Salerno and Anzio* (Eposition Press: New York, 1958)

Blumenson, Martin, *The Mediterranean Theatre of Operations: Salerno to Cassino* (US Government Printing Office: Washington DC, 1969)

Clark, Mark W., *Calculated Risk* (Harrap Publishing: New York, 1950)

Hickey, Des, and Smith, Gus, *Operation Avalanche: The Salerno Landings, 1943* (William Heinemann Ltd: London, 1983)

Graham, Dominic, and Bidwell, Shelford, *Tug of War: The Battle for Italy: 1943–45* (Hodder & Stoughton: London, 1986)

Konstam, Angus, *Salerno 1943: The Allied Invasion of Italy* (Pen & Sword: Barnsley, 2007)

Lamb, Richard, *War in Italy, 1943–45: A Brutal Story* (DaCapo Press: London, 1995)

Linklater, Eric, *The Campaign in Italy* (HMSO: London, 1951)

Mitchell, Raymond, *Marine Commando: Sicily and Salerno 1943 with 41 Royal Marines Commando* (Robert Hale Ltd.: London, 1988)

Molony, C. J. C., *Mediterranean and Middle East: Vol 5: Campaign in Sicily 1943 and the Campaign in Italy* (HMSO: London, 1973)

Morison, Samuel E., *History of the United States Naval Operations in World War II; Vol IX: Sicily-Salerno-Anzio, January 1943–June 1944* (Castle Books: New York, 1954)

Morris, Eric, *Salerno: A Military Fiasco* (Hutchinson & Co.: London, 1983)

Nelson, Guy, *A History of the 45th Infantry Division* (Oklahoma Publishing Company: Norman, OK, 1969)

Nelson, Harold M. (ed)., *Salerno: American Operations from the beaches to the Volturno, 9 September – 6 October 1943* (Center of Military History, United States Army: Washington DC, 1990)

Pond, Hugh, *Salerno* (Kimber Publishing: London, 1961)

Starr, Chester, *From Salerno to the Alps: A History of the Fifth Army, 1943–45* (Infantry Journal Press: Washington DC, 1948)

Wagner, Robert L., *The Texas Army: A History of the 36th Division in the Italian Campaign* (State House Press: Austin TX, 1969)

Werstein, Irving, *The Battle for Salerno* (Crowell Press: New York, 1965)